HISTORY AND GEOGRAPHY 1108
A NATION AT WAR

CONTENTS

Author: **Alpha Omega Staff**
Editor: Alan Christopherson M.S.
Illustrations: Alpha Omega Staff

Alpha Omega Publications®

804 N. 2nd Ave. E., Rock Rapids, IA 51246-1759

HISTORY 1108
A NATION AT WAR

The Depression that hit the United States during the early 1930s was not experienced by the United States alone. The effects of the economic disaster were felt world-wide and resulted in widespread hunger, unemployment, and desperation. Because of that desperation, some European nations built large military forces to combat the economic situation. As jobs became more numerous because of the increase in military troops, this build-up increased production and lowered unemployment. The subsequent military expansion, however, caused growing tensions as smaller nations were overcome by the threat of the great military power. This tension would eventually result in a second global confrontation, World War II. After the war, disputes over occupied territories gave way to a Cold War between the United States and the Soviet Union. Each nation sought the victory of its political philosophies on a world-wide scale. The eventual involvement of the United States in fighting the growth of Communism and totalitarianism throughout the world brought divisiveness and frustrations to its own people.

In this unit you will learn about the mounting tension on the European scene as nations overstocked their military might and sought to expand and to conquer. You will also examine the role of the United States and the strategies of the Allies in World War II on both the European and the Pacific fronts that ended in victory over the determined Axis powers. Next, you will observe how the Cold War between the United States and the Soviet Union arose over the occupation of nations following the war and how the Soviets later branched out with repeated outbreaks of Communist infiltration throughout the world. Also, you will learn why the United States assumed the role of "the world's policeman" against Communism and why it determined to help smaller nations against the threat of a Communist takeover. Finally, you will study the effect of the overseas involvement of the United States and the subsequent frustrations from the problems this involvement brought to America and its people.

Once steeped in isolationism, the United States stepped out boldly in the 1950s and 1960s to become the staunch opponent of Communism wherever it threatened the freedom of others. Hopefully, by studying this unit, you will better understand the price this country paid in terms of freedom—not only here but also for the freedom of people around the world.

OBJECTIVES

Read these objectives. The objectives tell you what you will be able to do when you have successfully completed this LIFEPAC®.

When you have finished this LIFEPAC, you should be able to:

1. Explain the economic and military causes of World War II.
2. Describe the Allied victories on the European front that led to the end of the war in Europe.
3. Describe the strategies and victories of the United States in the war on the Pacific front.
4. Identify the main issues and developments of the Cold War.
5. List the early offensives under President Truman and President Eisenhower against the growing communist threat.
6. Describe the causes and the hostilities of the Korean conflict.
7. Explain both the background and the influence of President Eisenhower in promoting world peace.
8. List the steps taken by President Kennedy in the United States' increased resistance against communist world infiltration.
9. Describe President Nixon's plan for withdrawal from Vietnam.
10. Describe the effects of the Vietnam war on United States servicemen and civilians.

Survey the LIFEPAC. Ask yourself some questions about this study. Write your questions here.

_____

_____

_____

_____

_____

_____

_____

_____

_____

_____

I. WORLD WAR II

The 1930s were years of desperate struggle for the citizens of the United States as they strove to keep their heads above the deep waters of the Great Depression. The positive actions of President Franklin D. Roosevelt had put a large number of people back to work and had inspired a discouraged United States. Economic recovery, however, had a long way to go to put the United States back on its feet. A world conflict played a major role.

World War II caused more deaths, cost more money, damaged more property, affected more people, and probably caused more far-reaching changes than any other war in history. The Second World War introduced the atomic age and brought sweeping changes in warfare. Trucks sped infantrymen to the battlefront after aerial bombings; giant tanks and pinpoint artillery weakened the enemy. Bombers and ballistic missiles rained death and destruction upon the armed forces and civilians alike. Airplanes, warships, and men worked together with split-second timing in **amphibious** attacks and paratroopers dropped from airplanes or landed in gliders to seek out the enemy.

The number of men killed, wounded or missing between September 1939 and September 1945, is impossible to accurately count. It is estimated that more than 10 million Allied troops and nearly 6 million Axis troops died during the Second World War. The war cost more than $1,000 trillion. More than fifty countries took part in the war with the entire world feeling the effects in one way or another. Fighting erupted in almost every part of the world. The chief battlefields of World War II were located in Asia, Europe, North Africa, the Atlantic Ocean, the Pacific Ocean, and both in and around the Mediterranean Sea.

World War II began on September 1, 1939 when Germany attacked Poland by using the _blitzkrieg_, or lightning warfare. Soon after this successful attack, the German war machine defeated Denmark, Norway, Belgium, Luxembourg, the Netherlands, and France. Surprisingly, the Germans required only three months to conquer these countries. However, Adolf Hitler, the dictator of Germany, failed in his prolonged attempt to defeat Great Britain with bombing missions and with submarine blockades. Nevertheless, by 1941 Hitler's armies had also conquered Yugoslavia and Greece and had marched into Soviet union.

Japan's plans for expansion in the Far East included a surprise attack on the United States' naval fleet at Pearl Harbor on December 7, 1941. Finally, after a series of serious disasters, the Allies took the offensive. Totally committed and determined, the Allies halted the Axis advances at El Alamein in North Africa, off Midway Island in the Pacific, and at Stalingrad in Soviet union. Allied amphibious invasions leapfrogged across the Pacific Islands and brought the Allies to the doorstep of Japan. In Europe, Allied troops landed in Italy and France and methodically pushed on into Germany. Italy surrendered on September 3, 1943; Germany surrendered on May 7, 1945; and, after the dropping of the atomic bomb on two Japanese cities, the Japanese surrendered on September 2, 1945, bringing an end to the terrible conflict known as World War II.

In this section you will study the economic and military causes of World War II and the factors that caused the United States to become involved in this global conflict.

SECTION OBJECTIVES

Review these objectives. When you have completed this section, you should be able to:

1.   Explain the economic and military causes of World War II:

    1.1   Describe the build-up of power in Germany, Italy, and Japan in the 1930s.

    1.2   Name two advantages of war on a nation's economy.

    1.3   Outline the seizure of land and power by the Germans and the Italians.

    1.4   Describe Japan's attack on Pearl Harbor.

2.   Describe the Allied victories on the European front that led to the end of the war in Europe.

3.   Describe the strategies and victories of the United States in the war on the Pacific front:

    3.1   Describe Doolittle's raid.

    3.2   Outline General MacArthur's strategies.

    3.3   Describe the bombing of Japan.

VOCABULARY

Study these words to enhance your learning success in this section.

amphibious	Debarking from ship to land
armada	A fleet of ships or large force of moving things
chancellor	In some European countries, a chief minister of state
dictator	One ruling absolutely and often oppressively
fascism	A political philosophy supporting an autocratic government headed by a dictator
Fuhrer	A title applied to Hitler by his followers; German for "leader"
guerrilla	Irregular fighting forces often operating at the rear of the enemy and using unconventional tactics
mobilize	To assemble and prepare for war or combat
premier	Chief minister of state
reprisal	The application of force by one nation against another in retaliation for acts committed

Note: All vocabulary words in this LIFEPAC appear in **boldface** print the first time they are used. If you are unsure of the meaning when you are reading, study the definitions given.

WORLD WAR II: CAUSES OF THE WAR

During the early 1930s Europe also felt the effects of the Great Depression. Hunger and unemployment were observed everywhere. In desperation the people of the Eastern Hemisphere, lacking strong leadership, capital, and equipment allowed things to occur that in better times they would have vigorously opposed. Hopelessly and tragically the people fell under the leadership of ruthless dictators and **fascism**.

AMPHIBIOUS ATTACK

Hitler

Mussolini

Economic causes. In Germany during the early 1930s, a sense of despair and helplessness prevailed. Germany's democratic tradition was deeply undermined when President Paul von Hindenburg asked Adolf Hitler to become **chancellor**. Many prominent Germans backed the appointment in hopes that this move would help to strengthen and to unite the country. As promised, Hitler did reduce unemployment. However, he accomplished this reduction by building up the military and by establishing various branches of his National Socialist Party's (Nazi) youth movement. Industrial jobs became numerous especially in factories producing military products. With the growth of industry, the economy improved. By building up its army, navy, and air force, the Germans were directly violating the Versailles Treaty that prohibited military growth. Hitler's ideas concerning the military were not confined to defensive purposes alone. A nation that banks its economy so heavily on its military strength becomes a dangerous nation that eventually requires an outlet such as war.

Meanwhile, in Italy, Benito Mussolini was in power as the **premier** and **dictator** from 1922 to 1943. Mussolini also limited unemployment by stressing military duty. Although not nearly as productive as German industry, the Italian economy was also based on a large military buildup, thus presenting another dangerous potential.

By the late 1930s Japan had also become more and more ambitious. For economic reasons, the Japanese were determined to take control of the various islands in southeast Asia. The natural resources of these islands, especially rubber and oil, were greatly needed by the Japanese. Control of these islands would also provide better trade and an advantage in fishing rights. With 90 million people living on four major islands and many smaller ones, Japan needed tremendous imported resources to fuel its modern industries. Because of a depressed economy and international politics, raw materials and trade in Japan were at dangerously low levels. The United States had created a sensitive situation with Japan because of the strong competition it was giving them in the race for natural resources and for increased Pacific trade.

4

Each of these nations—Germany, Italy, and Japan—desired and needed a better economic situation. Each nation put heavy emphasis on its military status. A military build-up would not be evil if it were used for defensive purposes; however, these nations had an ulterior purpose in mind. As their needs grew, their greed also grew. The trio used their strong military power to take the things they wanted by force. With the growth of military might, an unquenchable desire for power grew also. If Germany, Italy, and Japan had been patient, trade and commerce would have gradually improved their economic conditions. Unfortunately, some powerful nations operate on the theory that they can simply take whatever they need or want, especially from the weak.

The economy of the United States was growing slowly but steadily and, by the late 1930s, trade and commerce were rapidly developing. Though some of Franklin D. Roosevelt's programs failed, many turned out to be very successful. As the world moved toward the brink of war, however, the economies of the major nations reflected a surge in growth. As soldiers were **mobilized**, civilian jobs were left vacant for others and industry boomed in preparation for war. Not only were more jobs available, but numerous people were also called upon to work extra hours to meet production demands. That wars prevent depressions is an unfortunate truth, but is an economic fact. When World War II began in 1939, the world quickly pulled out of the Depression. Unfortunately, the disasters, sacrifices, and heartaches of such a global conflict for most would make the economic poverty of the Depression times seem like good years. As unemployment continued to drop, the United States was about to experience this economic phenomenon in the inevitable conflict to come; war pulled the United States out of the Great Depression.

Military causes. After President von Hindenburg died in 1934, both Germany and the world soon realized that Adolf Hitler was obsessed with a desire for personal power. After disposing of his opponents, the former Austrian wallpaper hanger, artist, and army corporal declared himself dictator.

Mussolini had led Italy with military-backed expansion techniques similar to Germany's. In October of 1935 Italian troops marched on Ethiopia. This defiant act by the Italians went unchecked by the European powers. The League of Nations could not even gather support for trade sanctions against Italy. The weak truly were at the mercy of the strong. The Ethiopians under Emperor Haile Selassie fought courageously; but their weapons were too few and too old. Mussolini's boast to make the Mediterranean Sea an "Italian lake" looked quite possible in the late 1930s.

By 1935 Hitler was publicly and blatantly breaking numerous restrictions imposed on Germany by the Versailles Treaty following World War I. His mobilization of the military and land stealing went unchallenged by other nations in Europe. Britain, France, and the Soviet Union did all they could to avoid the coming conflict with Germany. Yet the more Hitler was allowed to get away with, the bolder he became. Finally, after the Nazis seized Austria in 1938 and Czechoslovakia in 1939, the nations of Europe realized they had to resist with force or risk being swallowed up by the dictators one nation at a time. Something had to be done about this brazen aggression. It was the Germans invasion of Poland on September 1, 1939 that touched off the most devastating global war this world had ever seen. Though the Poles fought bravely with inferior weapons, they were soon defeated. The British, who had earlier signed an agreement to help Poland, declared war immediately. France soon joined Great Britain, but Italy later aligned with Hitler.

The last nation to join Italy and Germany in an alliance known as the Axis powers was Japan. Having a long history of aggression, Japan was already in a war with its archenemy, China. The hostilities ground to a deadlock on the mainland. Although the Japanese occupied major cities such as Beijing, Shanghai, and Canton, they could not totally defeat the Chinese. This Japanese failure resulted from the combined efforts of China's President Chiang Kai-shek in Western China and the Chinese Communist leader of **guerrilla** warfare, Mao Zedong.

As the Japanese watched the fighting in the European arena, they determined to turn the inevitable German victory to their profit. The Japanese furthered their expansion in the

5

Far East by invading additional island nations. Such moves brought protests from both the United States and the British. Japanese-American relations had been unsettled for some time, mainly because of their trade competition in the Pacific area. As Japanese diplomats met in Washington, D.C., to negotiate problems between the two countries, Japanese pilots were setting their sights on Pearl Harbor in the Hawaiian Islands where the naval power of the United States was based. The Hawaiian harbor held the strongest ships and air force support planes the United States possessed. On December 7, 1941, at 8:00 a.m., American sailors awoke to bombs and bullets, ironically, made of scrap iron from the United States.

DEC 7 1941

USS ARIZONA

USS WEST VIRGINIA
National Archives

National Archives

PEARL HARBOR

A balmy Sunday morning was turned into a black, smoke-filled nightmare for thousands of American servicemen. Over three thousand sailors and soldiers lay dead. Numerous ships and planes were left in smoking ruin. President Franklin Roosevelt, upon hearing of the attack, correctly stated that "this is a day that shall live in infamy."

Arguments for staying out of the war were now futile—the United States had no choice but to declare war on Japan. By an act of Congress on December 8, 1941, the United States went to war with the Empire of Japan and the nation was soon at war with Italy and Germany as well. With its navy crippled, the United States was poorly prepared for the naval battle that war with Japan would necessitate. Therefore, the United States entered the war at a distinct disadvantage, for adequate preparation often saves lives and builds both respect and confidence. As a large country in world affairs, this nation was woefully lacking all three aspects in December, 1941.

Complete the vocabulary matching.

1.1 _____ chancellor   a. Irregular fighting forces often operating at the rear of the enemy

1.2 _____ amphibious   b. One ruling absolutely and often oppressively

1.3 _____ dictator   c. Debarking from ship to land

1.4 _____ fascism   d. To assemble and prepare for war or combat

1.5 _____ guerrilla   e. A political philosophy supporting an autocratic government headed by a dictator

1.6 _____ mobilize   f. Chief minister of state

1.7 _____ premier   g. In some European countries, a chief minister of state

True/False.

1.8 _____ The German president in the 1930s was Paul von Hindenburg.

1.9 _____ Adolf Hitler was made chancellor of Germany by Mussolini.

1.10 _____ Benito Mussolini was the German emperor in the late 1930s.

1.11 _____ The German military build-up by Hitler violated the Versailles Treaty.

1.12 _____ The Italian economy, like the British, was centered around the military.

1.13 _____ The nation expanding its power in the western Pacific was Japan.

1.14 _____ The United States president in the 1930s was Theodore Roosevelt.

1.15 _____ War stimulates a nation's economy by increasing production and jobs.

Fill in the blank.

1.16 Hitler and Mussolini fought unemployment in their countries with _____ buildup.

1.17 Hitler broke the agreement set forth in the _____ Treaty from World War I with his build up of military power.

Choose the best answer(s).

1.18   Four reasons why Japan wanted control of the nearby Pacific islands were:

_____ a. access to rubber and oil

_____ b. to evangelize

_____ c. for a gift to Germany

_____ d. expansion

_____ e. improved trade

_____ f. fishing

1.19   Hitler was one of the following:

_____ a. a German president

_____ b. self-declared German dictator

_____ c. an army general

_____ d. afraid of power

1.20   Two countries seized by Hitler included:

_____ a. Poland

_____ b. Ethiopia

_____ c. China

_____ d. Austria

1.21   Three countries siding against Hitler's Germany were:

_____ a. Britain

_____ b. France

_____ c. Italy

_____ d. United States

Choose one answer.

1.22   The Axis powers included all except:

_____ a. China

_____ b. Italy

_____ c. Germany

_____ d. Japan

1.23   The Japanese:

_____ a. bombed San Francisco.

_____ b. felt hindered in trade by Britain.

_____ c. captured Hawaii.

_____ d. attacked Pearl Harbor.

1.24   Preparation for war:

_____ a. was a disadvantage of the United States in 1941

_____ b. prevents attacks

_____ c. destroys confidence

_____ d. was an advantage of the United States in 1941

Answer the following question.

1.25   What were the dangers in the military build-up of Germany, Italy and Japan?

_____

_____

_____

_____

_____

Adult Check _____

                 Initial   **Date**

WORLD WAR II: THEATERS OF OPERATION

The Germans seemed to be as surprised by Japan's sneak attack as the government of the United States. In fact, even after Japanese bombs had fallen on Pearl Harbor, the German foreign minister refused to believe the news was true. Instead, the Germans believed that the news of the attack was a propaganda trick of the enemy. Actually, Germany had hoped to keep the United States neutral; however, the Japanese changed all of that. At the urging of Japan, Hitler, and Mussolini both declared war on the United States on December 11, 1941. At that moment the United States found itself involved in a war against the Axis countries in two widely separated areas: on the European front and on the Pacific front.

European front. When the United States entered the war in Europe, the war had been under way for over two years. The first years at war had been very successful for the Germans. The German military machine was extremely efficient. In addition, the German soldiers were disciplined, well trained. They performed numerous outstanding and courageous feats. Most German soldiers, airmen, and sailors had strong military training as boys. Their lives were heavily influenced by Hitler's youth movement. Loyalty to the **Fuhrer** was instilled early in the lives of German youths. Although events would go badly for Germany later in the war, the military's loyalty remained true.

After Hitler's victories over Austria, Czechoslovakia, and Poland there was little action on the western front. Fighting was so infrequent, in fact, that the newspapers referred to the western battlefields as a phony war. A sudden German invasion of Denmark and Norway in April of 1940, however, ended such remarks. In addition, the Scandinavian conquests by Hitler jeopardized shipping between France and Great Britain. Not giving the Allies a chance to counteract, Germany immediately followed with the invasions of Holland, Belgium, and Luxembourg. The speed and power of the German attack was too devastating for the British forces, driving Great Britain off the European mainland and leaving the French to face Hitler alone. Seeing the French resistance weakening, Mussolini, who up to this time had kept Italy neutral, decided to side with Hitler and declared war on Britain and France. The attack on France came swiftly. France was poorly prepared for such an offensive and was forced to sign the Franco-German armistice in early June 1940, after the Germans victoriously entered Paris.

Now Britain was left to face Hitler alone. German bombing raids on the island of Britain were stepped up. Nevertheless, Britain–inspired by the invincible leadership of Winston Churchill–was determined to fight against the mounting odds, although the Germans urged them to accept a peaceful surrender. Militarily, the United States heavily supplied the British cause and gave the British as much support as possible without becoming involved in the actual fighting. Such increased involvement caused the United States to think more definitely in terms of preparing for war. Therefore, in September of 1940, the Selective Service Act established the military draft. Although many isolationists resisted it, most people in the United States realized the necessity of the draft in view of America's possible involvement in the war overseas.

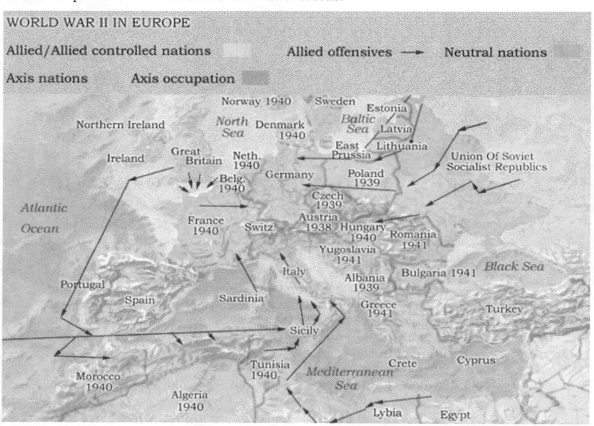

WORLD WAR II IN EUROPE

Allied/Allied controlled nations   Allied offensives →   Neutral nations

Axis nations   Axis occupation

Driven by his desire for power, Hitler set his sights on the control of the remaining Balkan states. To no one's surprise, the little countries of Romania and Bulgaria could not resist the powerful German offensives. In time, Yugoslavia and Greece also came under Axis control. The control of the Balkan states provided a launching point for the German campaigns waged against North Africa and the Middle East with its Suez Canal.

Germany had previously signed a nonaggressive pact with the Soviet Union (the communist name for the Russian empire) in which the two sides agreed to divide Poland. This gave Germany peace on their eastern front as the war escalated in the west. However, Hitler did not consider the pact binding. Consequently, in June of 1942, because of rising friction between the two nations, the Germans suddenly invaded the Soviet Union. This invasion engaged in battle the two largest armies in the world. The Russians, fought the German assault with **guerrilla** warfare, fighting defensively, retreating, and burning anything of value as they went. This brutal resistance slowed the German invasion until the bitter Russian winter set in and halted the Germans advance. Taking advantage of this respite and their superior preparation for winter warfare, the Russians counterattacked and drove the Germans back. The Germans ended the year, nevertheless, deep in Soviet territory. With their army still in good shape the Germans hoped to be able to fight their kind of war again in the spring. However, the spring of 1942 brought a new power to the war arena–the United States of America.

Following the disaster of Pearl Harbor, Congress declared war on Japan. Germany and Italy then declared war on the United States and Great Britain declared war on Japan. By the time the United States entered the conflict, Italy had no significant role in the fighting. Italians did not excel in combat and quite often their lack of dependability resulted in more problems than help to the Germans.

The United States had been supplying the Allied powers of Great Britain, France, and the Soviet Union with the necessary arms and supplies from the beginning of the conflict. When the United States finally committed itself to send troops to Europe in 1942, the complexion of the war began to change. In November of 1942 United States soldiers led by General Dwight D. Eisenhower landed in North Africa. The United States joined the British in driving out the Germans, although the Germans were led shrewdly by Field Marshall Rommel. By May of 1943 two hundred fifty thousand German soldiers were taken prisoner along with their supplies and equipment. Moreover, the German war machine had finally been halted in the east by the Soviet army in Stalingrad at the end of 1942.

Italy became another battleground for the fierce fighting of Allied and Axis powers. When the Italian army was driven out of the war, divisions of crack German troops rushed to stop the Allied advance following their retreat. The American troops fought bravely and courageously on the battlefields of Italy. Bloody engagements took place at Anzio, Salerno, Palermo, and other spots in southern Italy. American men gained a reputation of being good soldiers with a fighting spirit–a resurrection of the same spirit shown at Valley Forge, the Alamo, Gettysburg, and Chateau-Thierry. Although not wanting war, the United States rose to the occasion when it was threatened or whenever and wherever injustices occurred.

Troops Landing at Normandy

By 1944 the Germans still offered stubborn resistance. Since Germany controlled much of Europe, a tremendous effort by the Allies would be necessary to drive the Germans back to the Rhine River. After Great Britain's prime minister, Sir Winston Churchill and President Franklin D. Roosevelt conferred, General Dwight D. Eisenhower was appointed to lead an Allied invasion of occupied France. American ships, airplanes, equipment, and servicemen would be the major part of this task force–and what a task it would be to conquer the Nazis at such a strategic position. The French coastline was heavily fortified by the Germans who were expecting an invasion. Many of Germany's best troops were held in reserve just waiting for such an eventuality.

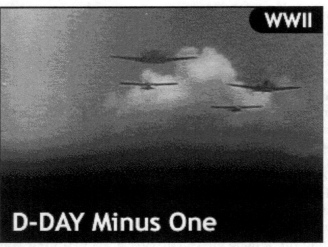

D-DAY Minus One

Plans were finalized to liberate France in June of 1944. Allied soldiers, sailors, and airmen trained long, diligently, and thoroughly for their assignments. Casualties were expected to be extremely high. The importance of knowing and carrying out individual duties was strongly stressed. The fewer mistakes made in the operation, the fewer men would die.

As invasion time neared, the Allied forces gathered in Great Britain. Bad weather made it difficult for General Eisenhower and his advisors to choose the date on which to launch their tremendous offensive. Finally, with a fifty-fifty chance of fair weather, the choice of June 6 was made by General Eisenhower. Hopefully, the good vision needed so desperately by the airplanes would be available. The possibility of a successful landing even with good weather, however, was questionable. The chosen site at Normandy Beach, in northern France, was also disputed by military experts, but the plans were already set. Now only time would tell the wisdom of these decisions.

D-DAY

Shortly after midnight, planes began leaving Great Britain for the coast of France. Vital supplies were dropped for the coming invaders. Many members of the French underground received airdrops to carry out sabotage assignments that included blowing up railroad tracks, cutting telephone wires, and kidnapping German sympathizers. Thousands of fake "paratroopers" were dropped to confuse the armies of Hitler—miniature dummies that exploded on impact gave the impression of an air invasion miles from Normandy. These diversion tactics were performed well. Early on the morning of June 6, the German high command was still confused as to where and when the invasion would take place.

In addition, United States paratroopers were also dropped behind enemy lines to help French underground forces and to capture strategic targets, such as small towns, railroad stations, and key geographical locations. Because of the nighttime conditions and the inclement weather, pilots had trouble pinpointing the drop zones for the soldiers. Many troops landed miles from where they were supposed to meet. Units became mixed, but commanders did their utmost to make the best of the situation. One unit actually landed in the town they were supposed to capture by surprise and German soldiers shot most of the paratroopers as they came down. Amazingly, however, many of the planned objectives were actually carried out. The airborne soldiers also caused a tremendous amount of confusion and harassment by their unexpected landing.

United States and British commandos fared even worse than the paratroopers. They were to land behind the German lines in gliders the night before the dawn invasion. However, most of the gliders could not find clearings to land and had to crash. Many of the commandos were severely injured on impact. However, the commandos were well-trained combat specialists who performed responsibilities similar to the paratroopers and the

French underground, but with much more difficulty and risk involved. Those commandos who remained uninjured helped make the invasion of Normandy a success.

At dawn on June 6, the skepticism, doubt, fears, and assertions of the German military command came to an end. Debates were no longer needed concerning the location and the time of the invasion. The hundreds of planes that began bombing French coastal targets and the numerous ships seen on the horizon of the English Channel settled the issue. The world has never seen anything as awesome as this Allied **armada**.

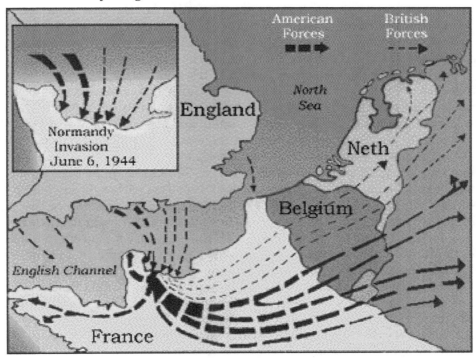

Although the Germans offered stiff resistance and inflicted heavy casualties upon the Allies, the landing was a hard-fought success. War in Europe would last another year with plenty of bitter fighting, but the triumph of the Normandy invasion was the seal of doom for Hitler and his army.

From Normandy's beaches the Allies started a drive across France and into Germany. At the same time, the Soviets closed in on the Germans from the east. Many Nazi generals fled the country and Hitler committed suicide. After six long and grueling years, the war in Europe finally came to an end on May 8, 1945. Though millions celebrated V-E Day, the horrors of the European conflict would be forgotten neither easily nor quickly.

Not only were hundreds of thousands of servicemen killed in the war, but also thousands of civilians met their deaths in the bombings from both sides. Also revealed at the end of the war was the brutal annihilation of six million Jews, who were captured and killed by the Nazis at various concentration camps in Europe. Such Nazi actions demanded severe measures and were ultimately condemned at a series of trials held at Nuremberg, Germany, immediately after the war. Although numerous German officers were tried as war criminals for these abominable acts, many of them escaped to North and South America before they were brought to justice.

Pacific front. Following the panic set off by the Japanese sneak attack on Pearl Harbor, the United States immediately established a defensive policy in the Pacific. No Allied movement against Japan existed like the one in Europe against the Germans; therefore, the United States had to start at the bottom in an uphill battle in the Pacific. Panic spread throughout California and its neighboring Western states, in fear that a Japanese invasion might take place at any time. In an assuring move, much of the nation's defensive efforts concentrated on patrolling this country's west coast. Eventually the British came to the aid of the United States along with some Australian and Chinese support, but the bulk of the operation in Eastern Asia fell upon the United States. Fortunately, the Pacific front allowed the United States time to gather and to train the men needed to defeat the menacing military power of Japan. The slogan, "Remember Pearl Harbor," lived in the hearts of American citizens and did not cease until V-J (Victory in Japan) Day.

The Japanese high command wasted little time following Pearl Harbor with immediate orders to invade numerous other Pacific islands. With the United States Navy nearly crippled by the attack, Japan successfully invaded much of the western Pacific and Eastern Asia. These Japanese successes included Guam and Wake islands and the cities of Manila and Singapore.

The only place to hold out against the onslaught for any length of time was the peninsula of Bataan and the island fortress of Corregidor in the Philippines. They were defended by an American army with Filipino support under General Douglas MacArthur. However, the men were short of supplies and the U.S. had no way to send relief. It was only a matter of time. The Japanese took Bataan in April of 1942 and Corregidor the following month. Sixty thousand American and Filipino prisoners–many already weak from disease and malnutrition–were forced to march seventy miles. Less than fifty thousand reached the Japanese prison camp in what was called the Bataan Death March. Their Japanese captors had shot or bayoneted those prisoners who fell out of the line of march due to wounds, disease or fatigue.

General Douglas MacArthur was chosen to lead the United States military in the Pacific region. After spending many years in the Philippine Islands, MacArthur was well experienced in dealing with the Japanese and other Asians. General MacArthur had to leave the Philippine Islands in 1942, however, and to relocate his headquarters in Brisbane, Australia. MacArthur vowed to return to the Philippines and promised the people, "I shall return." During his absence, some of the bloodiest battles in the history of warfare were fought. True to his words, the general did return in 1945.

While the United States was still reeling from the unexpected blow at Pearl Harbor, its military leaders were desperately planning a retaliatory strike upon the Japanese. The strike had to come early and it had to be successful since the morale of the United States desperately needed a lift. After discussing several possibilities, the decision was made to bomb Tokyo. Japan's leaders were obstinate, proud, and arrogant. Such a feat would shock them, but more importantly, it would lift America's dirt low morale.

President Roosevelt wanted the raid of **reprisal** to take place as soon as possible. Lieutenant Colonel James H. Doolittle was chosen to lead the attack on Tokyo. Sixteen planes would bomb Tokyo and three other Japanese cities, taking off from a naval aircraft carrier that would transport the bombers as close to Japan as possible without being detected. On the morning of April 18, 1942, at 7:20 a.m., Doolittle's plane lifted off the carrier *Hornet* and headed for Tokyo. The remaining fifteen planes followed to the cheers of the navy crew on the deck.

The raid was even more of a surprise to the Japanese than Pearl Harbor was to the United States. Continuous propaganda had assured residents of Tokyo that United States planes could not possibly bomb their homeland. This idea was based on the theory that United States planes would have to be within four hundred miles of Japan before they could be launched from aircraft carriers. Since the Japanese surveillance system covered up to seven hundred miles, the Japanese reasoned that they would have plenty of time to stop an attack.

Although the *Hornet* was probably detected before it reached six hundred miles off the coast, its B-25 bombers got off without incident. Doolittle was ordered to leave a day earlier than planned. Not only did this change in plans eliminate the important cover of darkness, it also jeopardized the mission's chances because of the additional gas needed since every ounce would count. When Admiral William F. Halsey wished Doolittle well and added, "God bless you," Halsey became a prophet and the smoothness with which the operation took place was clear evidence of God's sovereignty and blessing. The attack was carried out without a single plane being shot down.

Although the planned landing spot in Asia could not be reached because of a lack of gasoline, most of the raiding party parachuted to safety and were picked up by the Chinese. Only one plane crashed killing its crew, and another crew parachuted into Japanese-held territory where they were taken prisoner. From a military standpoint Doolittle's raid was not very significant; however, the raid did provide an important psychological lift to the United States.

The Pacific campaign was largely a naval one with the United States marines doing most of the land fighting. Following major naval and air battles during the first six months of 1942, the United States planned a series of island-hopping conquests that would lead them just short of Japan.

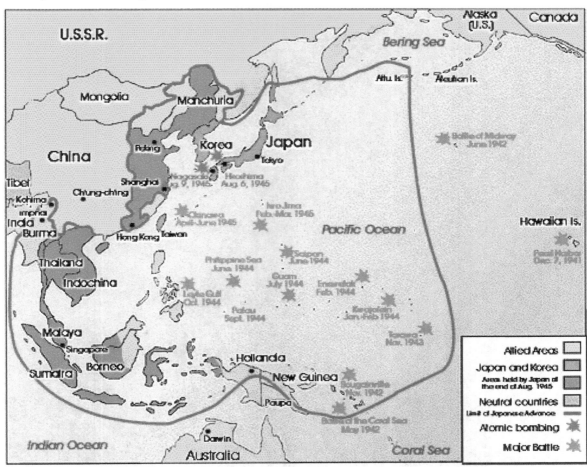

This island-hopping strategy began after the air victory at the Battle of the Coral Sea in May of 1942 which stopped a Japanese invasion of southern New Guinea. The Battle of Guadalcanal, off Australia's northeastern coast, began on August 7, 1942, marking the beginning of the United States marine assaults on the occupied islands. Fierce battles were fought on Guadalcanal and many United States marines were killed in action.

Soldier at Guadalcanal

Following Guadalcanal were the battles of the Solomon Islands, New Guinea, New Britain, Tarawa, Guam, and Saipan. Crucial victories that combined air and sea forces in the battles of the Philippine Sea and Leyte Gulf in 1944 led to the Americans landing in the Philippines in 1945. Two more famous battles soon followed at Iwo Jima and Okinawa. The historic picture of the group of marines raising the United States flag was taken on Iwo Jima in March of 1945. By June of that year, Okinawa fell to the United States forces.

15

Then the Allied effort was on the verge of total victory. British and Australian troops fought alongside American sailors, soldiers, airmen, and marines in making this victory possible. Before total victory in the Pacific could be achieved, however, the United States still had to conquer Japan and Japan was expected to be a formidable enemy. The Japanese believed it was an honor to die in battle for their country and their emperor. This thinking led thousands of Japanese pilots to become human bombs as they crashed into United States ships while strapped into their airplanes. These Kamikaze fliers, along with like minded Japanese soldiers and tropical diseases threatened the United States forces during the Pacific campaign.

IWO JIMA

By the spring of 1945, General MacArthur and his advisors were considering the invasion of Japan's mainland. Casualties were expected to run into the hundreds of thousands; therefore, the decision to invade was carefully studied and evaluated. Finally, when General MacArthur met with President Truman—sworn into office following Franklin Roosevelt's death in 1944—and diplomats from the United States and Great Britain, an unexpected decision was made. The recently developed atomic bomb would be used. One bomb would be dropped on Hiroshima on August 6 and another on Nagasaki on August 9, 1945.

The dropping of these two bombs will remain controversial. The devastation of Hiroshima and Nagasaki brought surrender of the Japanese on August 10, 1945. Although thousands of people were killed or maimed by the bombs, many people have argued that the bombing was necessary. The cost in Allied and Japanese lives would have been far greater

16

had an invasion of Japan taken place. Also, the bombs would serve as a deterring factor in checking the rising Communist threat of world dominion that was growing at the end of World War II.

By the time V-J Day arrived on September 2, the United States was ready for peace. Four years of fighting had drained the country's manpower, leaving many people weary of war and in search of peace. A feeling of satisfaction and a spirit of confidence spread quickly throughout this nation. World War II had given the world's free countries an awful scare. The war took a tremendous national and Allied effort to put down the totalitarian Axis powers. The war was over, however, and the dreadful price for this country's security had been paid. Although scars from the second global conflict were obvious on every hand, they would slowly fade with the healing power of time.

Match the following with the correct definition.

1.26 _____ Fuhrer

1.27 _____ reprisal

1.28 _____ armada

a. A fleet of ships or large force of moving things

b. The application of force by one nation against another in retaliation for acts committed

c. A title applied to Hitler by his followers

Follow the directions.

1.29 Describe the overall strategy involved in defeating the Germans in Europe–where the Allies began and where they ended.

_____
_____
_____
_____
_____

1.30 Describe the effect the weather had on the Allied Forces in the Battle of Normandy.

_____
_____
_____
_____
_____

Adult Check _____

Initial   **Date**

Choose the best answer(s).

1.31   An unsuccessful German offensive of 1940 was the:

_____ a. invasion of Great Britain

_____ b. takeover of Denmark and Norway

_____ c. invasion of France

_____ d. invasion of Holland and Belgium

1.32   An opponent of Great Britain during the war was:

_____ a. France

_____ b. Italy

_____ c. the Soviet Union

_____ d. United States

1.33   A factor hindering the German invasion of the Soviet Union was:

_____ a. Italian warfare

_____ b. a mild winter

_____ c. Soviet guerrilla warfare

_____ d. British reinforcements

1.34   What two allied military actions began to take the punch out of Germany's power?

_____ a. their conquest of North Africa

_____ b. the Japanese attack on Pearl Harbor

_____ c. the halting of Hitler's armies by the Soviet Union

_____ d. Italy's strong fighting force

_____ e. quick takeover of Romania and Bulgaria

1.35   What three nations were allies of the United States in the war with Japan?

_____ a. Britain

_____ b. France

_____ c. Australia

_____ d. China

_____ e. the Soviet Union

1.36   Three islands seized by Japan included:

_____ a. Guam

_____ b. Corregidor

_____ c. Crete

_____ d. Wake

_____ e. Hawaii

1.37   Two last-minute problems in the American attack on Tokyo were:

_____ a. had to attack in daylight

_____ b. not enough gas

_____ c. Japan found out about the attack

Match these leaders of World War II.

1.38 _____ Rommel   a. United States president

1.39 _____ Churchill   b. German dictator

1.40 _____ Eisenhower   c. German commander of North African forces

1.41 _____ Hitler   d. Italian dictator

1.42 _____ Mussolini   e. British Prime Minister

1.43 _____ Roosevelt   f. the commander of Allied invasion of France

True/False.

1.44 _____ Allied forces gathered in Britain for the Battle of Normandy.

1.45 _____ The Battle of Normandy began June 6, 1945.

1.46 _____ The Second World War in Europe ended May 8, 1945.

1.47 _____ German war criminals were tried at Nuremberg, France.

1.48 _____ The American commander in the Pacific was General MacArthur.

1.49 _____ The bombing attack on Tokyo was led by Doolittle.

1.50 _____ The Pacific battles were mainly land battles.

1.51 _____ Ground fighting in the Pacific was led by the United States marines.

1.52 _____ The Japanese surrendered on August 10, 1944.

1.53 _____ The attack on Tokyo surprised the Japanese because they were told the U.S. planes could not get close without detection.

Adult Check _____

            Initial   **Date**

Review the material in this section in preparation for the Self Test. The Self Test will check your mastery of this particular section. The items missed on this Self Test will indicate specific areas where restudy is needed for mastery.

SELF TEST 1

Match these items (each answer, 2 points).

1.01 _____ Paul von Hindenburg   a. Italian dictator

1.02 _____ Adolf Hitler   b. United States president

1.03 _____ Benito Mussolini   c. British prime minister

1.04 _____ Franklin Roosevelt   d. American general in Pacific

1.05 _____ Haile Selassie   e. German president

1.06 _____ Dwight Eisenhower   f. the Fuhrer

1.07 _____ Rommel   g. Ethiopian emperor

1.08 _____ Winston Churchill   h. an Allied general of the Battle of Normandy

1.09 _____ Douglas MacArthur   i. German Field Marshall

1.010 _____ James Doolittle   j. American commander of Tokyo attack

True/False (each answer, 1 point).

1.011 _____ The Treaty of Versailles was violated by Hitler's military build up.

1.012 _____ Mussolini's National Socialist Party's youth movement instilled loyalty in Germany's youth.

1.013 _____ Eisenhower and his men drove the Italians from North Africa.

1.014 _____ The Allied powers were made up of Italy, Germany, and Japan.

1.015 _____ The Japanese attacked Pearl Harbor on December 9, 1941.

1.016 _____ Japan seized Pacific islands to boost its economy and trade.

1.017 _____ Bad weather hindered the Allied attack on Normandy.

1.018 _____ The war in Europe came to an end May 8, 1945.

1.019 _____ Britain, Australia, and France aided the United States in the war against Japan.

1.020 _____ The bombing of Tokyo was a much needed morale booster for the United States.

Fill in the blanks (each answer, 3 points).

1.021 Germany, Italy, and Japan based their economies upon _____.

1.022 World War II helped the American economy recover from the effects of the

_____ .

1.023 Mussolini fought Selassie for control of _____ .

1.024   Countries siding with Britain against Hitler were:

_____

_____

_____

1.025   Churchill and Roosevelt appointed _____ to lead the Normandy invasion.

1.026   The Allies closed in on Germany from the west and the _____ moved in on them from the east.

1.027   The Bataan Death March followed the Japanese seizure of _____ .

1.028   United States' troops in the Pacific were led by General _____ .

1.029   Japanese _____ pilots crashed into United States ships.

1.030   Atomic bombs were dropped on Hiroshima and _____ .

Choose the best answer(s) (each answer, 2 points).

1.031   Germany, Italy, and Japan built up their militaries to: _____ .
         a. slow down the economy
         b. trade with the West
         c. beat one another
         d. increase their power

1.032   Hitler soon spread his destructive power to: _____ .
         a. Ethiopia
         b. Poland
         c. Mexico
         d. China

1.033   The Allied commander in Europe in World War II was: _____ .
         a. Eisenhower
         b. Doolittle
         c. Churchill
         d. MacArthur

1.034   Attacks behind enemy lines in the Battle of Normandy were led by: _____ .
         a. the French army
         b. German sympathizers
         c. American paratroopers
         d. Italians

1.035   What did the United States use in the attack on Japan in 1945 to end the war? _____
         a. Doolittle's raid
         b. atomic bombs
         c. Pacific island hopping
         d. the invasion of Japan by foot

1.036   War and military build-up help the economy of a country by lowering: _____ .
a. unemployment
b. taxes
c. production
d. inflation

1.037   Two advantages Hitler and Mussolini had over nearby countries were: _____ , _____
a. military strength
b. stronger nationalism
c. modern weapons
d. greater intelligence

1.038   The reasoning behind America's decision to drop atomic bombs on Japan was that: _____ .
a. it would save lives
b. the war could not be won without it
c. the Japanese deserved it
d. there were no other options

Follow the directions (this answer 4 points).

1.039   Describe the overall strategy involved in defeating the Germans in Europe–where the Allies began and where they ended.

_____

_____

_____

_____

_____

70
88

Score
Adult Check

_____

_____

Initial   **Date**

II. KOREAN CONFLICT

Following World War II, a spirit of optimism prevailed in the United States similar to that following the First World War. With the military threats of Germany and Japan no longer a problem, the safety of this nation and the world seemed assured indefinitely. If a lasting peace had not been earned after four long years of American involvement in the war, at least hostilities were not expected to erupt in the near future. Like so many wishes and good intentions, however, such optimistic thinking was soon to be quickly shattered.

In this section you will study the reaction of the free world to the mounting Communist threat. You will also study the formation of two peace-keeping organizations: the United Nations and the North Atlantic Treaty Organization (NATO).

SECTION OBJECTIVES

Review these objectives. When you have completed this section, you should be able to:

4. Identify the main issues and developments of the Cold War:

    4.1 Examine the question of occupation in conquered areas of World War II.

    4.2 Outline the formation of the United Nations.

5. List the early offensives under President Truman and President Eisenhower against the growing communistic threat:

    5.1 Explain the Truman Doctrine.

    5.2 Explain the Marshall Plan.

    5.3 Describe the Berlin airlift.

    5.4 Examine the North Atlantic Treaty Organization.

6. Describe the causes and the hostilities of the Korean conflict.

7. Explain the background and the influence of President Eisenhower in promoting world peace.

VOCABULARY

Study these words to enhance your learning success in this section.

Kuomintang	The Chinese Nationalist Party led by Chiang Kai-shek.
ratified	Made valid by approving; confirmed.

COMMUNIST THREAT: WORLD UNREST

WORLD UNREST DEMANDS ACTION

The security earned in defeating Germany and the other Axis powers was short-lived in the postwar years. Following V-E Day in Europe and V-J Day in the Pacific, world peace was almost immediately threatened. The frequently used term, "the hot war," a term used to describe actual fighting, was soon to be traded for what came to be known as "the Cold War." The process of rebuilding Europe and Japan after the destruction of the Second World War was underway. The threat of Communism, however, advanced as the Soviets spread their influence and propaganda through Eastern Europe and parts of Asia.

Postwar effects. During the difficult years of World War II, other major issues demanded the consideration of the Allied powers besides the numerous problems of the hot war. One of these issues would later mushroom into a Cold War. The Cold War would foster hostilities between nations with resulting diplomatic moves and with political decisions as complex and as intense as any war of bullets and bombs. Because of the tension of the hot war itself, the Cold War issues grew steadily and insidiously behind the scene, drawing little publicity and attention. One especially volatile issue concerned Allied occupation of certain conquered areas. As Europe was the arena of much of the fighting in World War II, the question of occupation of certain European countries was particularly intense.

The United States, Great Britain, and the Soviet Union soon emerged as the primary adversaries in this behind-the-scenes struggle. The United States and Great Britain had no imperialistic motives for entering the Second World War. Their main objectives were to defend themselves and to reestablish peaceful stability throughout the world, while strongly encouraging a philosophy of each nation determining its own future. Although the United States and Great Britain did not intend to actively seek out newly conquered lands to expand their own domains, they were determined to defend the right of these lands to be free from aggressive interference of any oppressive outsiders.

The Soviet Union, on the other hand, had opposing ideas. The bitter hatred that had existed between Russia and Germany for many years greatly influenced Soviet thinking. The Soviets were invaded in both the first and the second world wars by the Germans and were determined that invasion would not happen again. The Soviets sought occupation of as much of the German land as possible. This occupation would provide an excellent deterrent, in their opinion, to repeated German offenses.

On August 14, 1941 President Franklin D. Roosevelt and Prime Minister Winston Churchill signed the famous Atlantic Charter, stressing that neither country wanted to acquire territory nor would attempt to govern other nations. In sincerely stating their policy, the United States and Great Britain wished to make their positions clear not only to Germany and the Axis powers but also to the Soviet Union. Meanwhile, the Soviets made clear that they had no intention of giving up any territories they had gained during the war. True to their cause, by the end of World War II, Russia not only insisted on remaining in conquered areas, but also demanded final say on the running of those governments. The Soviet occupied nations of Eastern Europe were forced to become communist.

The international arena following World War II dictated at least an attempt to form an organization where representatives from around the world could meet and resolve their differences. Hopefully, the organization would be stronger than the League of Nations which

The United Nations

24

never had either the support of the United States or the power to carry out international objectives. In order to be effective, any international organization formed would have to include both the Soviet Union and the United States.

On April 25, 1945 representatives of fifty nations, including the Soviet Union and the United States, met in San Francisco to form the United Nations. An assembly was established that included representatives from every nation, the formation of a Security Council of major countries and the appointment of a Secretary General. To deal with various problems that might arise, additional committees and councils were also provided in the United Nations Charter.

Unlike the League of Nations, which Woodrow Wilson so desperately fought to establish, the United Nations was wholly supported by the people of the United States, their representatives in government and by President Harry S. Truman. Realizing that for the United States isolationism was a thing of the past, the United States Senate **ratified** the agreement 89-2 on June 28, 1945. The test of time would show how effectively the United Nations would function. It must be kept in mind, however, that whatever their political maneuverings, most countries wanted to avoid war if at all possible. Two global wars just twenty years apart had taught the nations of the world a bitter lesson they did not wish to repeat soon.

Soviet greed. Western world leaders soon realized that it would take much more than the United Nations to halt the huge Soviet appetite. The Soviets wanted to control conquered countries in Eastern Europe and also to seek new lands to devour.

National Archives

Harry S. Truman

In July of 1945, President Harry Truman, Prime Minister Winston Churchill and Premier Joseph Stalin met at Potsdam, a city in East Germany, to discuss the future of occupied European countries. The Soviets as well as the French were absolutely unyielding in their argument against the complete unification of Germany. Having been invaded by the Germans twice in less than half a century was experience enough for both the Soviet Union and France to know that a unified Germany could not be trusted. A decision was finally reached by the Big Three leaders not only to disarm Germany and to cut back the number of occupying troops but also to develop a democratic method of government in Germany and to bring justice to the leaders of the Nazi party.

The talks at Potsdam and later negotiations in London clearly forecast the difficult future ahead for the United States and Great Britain in reasoning with the Soviets. The choice was almost always "do it Russia's way or not at all!" Attitudes were quite strong in discussing the fate of German industry also. The Soviets wanted German industry stalled and reduced to unproductive levels indefinitely, whereas Great Britain and the United States believed in a limited use for non-military purposes.

However, the postwar trials of former Nazis was easily agreed upon and were set to be held in Nuremberg, Germany. On October 11, 1946, international trials found twelve Nazis guilty of war crimes punishable by death. Lesser trials continued for some years searching out less prominent members of the Nazi party.

Both the United States and Great Britain realized the necessity of negotiating with the Soviet Union immediately, before the great bulk of military men returned home from Europe. The Soviets would have a definite bargaining advantage because of their large military build-up in Eastern Germany and in other sections of Eastern Europe.

In the United States many citizens were demanding a hard line and a "get-tough" policy from the Truman administration concerning Soviet relations. The citizens of the United States, concerned about what Stalin and his Communist regime were trying to do, thought this country's government representatives were being too soft in their dealings with the Soviets. The future of millions of Europeans who were faithful to American, British, and even Soviet causes were now at stake in the issue. The United States tradition of supporting the weak and the helpless came through loud and clear at this crucial time in the history of Europe and of the world.

For a while Europe appeared to be bracing for yet another war. The Soviet Union was increasing its boasts and its propaganda of Communist superiority. While the United States and British military forces were gradually reduced following the war, the Soviets maintained their troops at full wartime strength of more than six million.

By 1947 with international tension mounting and with growing unrest at home, President Truman knew that firm action was needed immediately. A situation soon arose that caused President Truman to take that action. Greece was in the midst of a revolution led by the Communists. At the same time, Turkey was insecure about being left without the strong military support that the British had supplied. The Turks, situated on the Soviet Union's border, were particularly vulnerable to a Soviet takeover. In March of 1947, President Truman asked and received from Congress $400 million in military and economic support for Greece and Turkey beginning what became known as the Truman Doctrine, a declaration that the United States would support countries committed to taking a stand against Communism. The aid helped those nations avoid being taken over by communism. Furthermore, President Truman's actions led to the establishment of the Marshall Plan.

George C. Marshall, Secretary of State at the time, first announced his program at Harvard University in June of 1947. It was approved by Congress in 1948. The Marshall Plan put the responsibility of a nation's economic future on the country itself. Avoiding the ideological differences between Communistic and democratic societies, aid was offered to any nation willing to adhere to the program. Proving to be overwhelmingly successful in the late 1940s and early 1950s, the Marshall Plan was a tremendous positive force in containing the challenge of Communism. It helped the free nations of Europe rebuild their economies so their nations were secure against communist ideas.

The Soviet Union refused to allow occupied Germany to be reunited as a free nation in the years after the war. In 1948 Great Britain, France, and the United States decided to allow the parts of Germany they occupied to unite and form a separate country of their own, West Germany. The Soviets responded by blockading the roads leading into West Berlin, the part of the capital held by the western powers. (Berlin was completely inside the Soviet occupied part of Germany.) The response of the Allies was the famous Berlin Airlift, whereby the city was supplied by American and British airplanes until the blockade was called off in 1949.

With so many European nations feeling the threat of the Soviet Bear, these nations counteracted by joining with other countries to form the North Atlantic Treaty Organization (NATO) on April 4, 1949. Those nations whose representatives signed the pact were Belgium, Canada, Denmark, Great Britain, France, Iceland, Italy, Luxembourg, the Netherlands, Norway, Portugal, and the United States. According to the NATO agreement, any attack against one of these nations would be considered an attack against all of them. Officially the pact went into effect on August 24, 1949 with the establishing of their headquarters in Paris.

NATO had committed the United States to a defense of Western Europe against a Soviet attack. Thus, not only was this nation instrumental in Western Europe's postwar recovery economically, but also it assured their military security. The goals of containing Communism in Europe now had some structure. Strong statements by governmental leaders, such as Secretary of State Dean Acheson, in the early 1950s emphasized the determination of the United States not to allow the Iron Curtain, the border between communist and free Europe, to advance. Although this country accepted a grave responsibility, the responsibility was absolutely necessary in view of the United States' own defense against Soviet aggression.

HISTORY & GEOGRAPHY

1 1 0 8

LIFEPAC TEST

80 / 100

HISTORY AND GEOGRAPHY 1108 LIFEPAC TEST

Match these items (each answer, 2 points).

1. _____ Normandy   a. Japanese bombing attack on the United States Navy

2. _____ Pearl Harbor   b. atomic bomb site, ended the war in the Pacific

3. _____ Nagasaki   c. Allied attack beginning takeover of France

4. _____ United Nations   d. an organization giving Asian nations defense against a Communist threat

5. _____ NATO   e. a resolution giving Johnson authority to retaliate militarily in Vietnam

6. _____ SEATO   f. an organization giving European nations defense against a Communist threat

7. _____ Gulf of Tonkin   g. the Cuban invasion that attempted to overthrow Castro

8. _____ Cold War   h. determined the future of occupied nations following World War II

9. _____ Marshall Plan   i. financial aid to European nations

10. _____ Bay of Pigs   j. an organization for solving world problems peacefully

11. _____ Potsdam meetings   k. withdrawal of United States troops from Vietnam

12. _____ Vietnamization   l. bloodless conflict between United States and the Soviets

True/False (each answer, 1 point).

13. _____ Hitler and Mussolini headed the Axis powers of World War II.

14. _____ Doolittle's raid raised hopes for an American victory in the Pacific.

15. _____ Mao Zedong headed the Communist forces in Vietnam; Chiang Kai-shek headed the Nationalists.

16. _____ Kennedy's cautious firmness with Khrushchev during the Cuban missile crisis resulted in the disassembling of Soviet missiles sites.

17. _____ Eisenhower, Kennedy, and Johnson all approved of the United States backing the South Vietnamese in their civil war.

18. _____ Ho Chi Minh led the Communist forces in Indochina and in North Vietnam.

19. _____ The Truman-MacArthur conflict concerned all-out war in Indochina.

20. _____ Hitler's power in Europe was seriously checked when the United States entered the war.

21. _____ The Atlantic Charter demonstrated American imperialism after World War II.

22. _____ Drugs, immorality, and lack of respect for the military and government became national problems after Vietnam.

Fill in the blanks (each answer, 3 points).

23. The calling of soldiers into active duty is called _____ .

24. American rehabilitation programs sought to restore soldiers to good health who had fought in _____ .

25. General MacArthur led the American forces in World War II on the _____ front.

26. The United States became actively involved in Vietnam combat during the administration of President _____ .

27. Kissinger was Secretary of State under President _____ .

28. France, the United States, the Soviet Union, and Great Britain composed the _____ forces during _____ .

29. Italy and Germany were known as the _____ powers during World War II.

30. The commander of the Allied forces on the European front during World War II was General _____ .

31. Some United States citizens reacted against continued involvement in Vietnam through _____ marches.

Choose the best answer(s) (each answer, 2 points).

32. Allied strategy on the European front in World War II included five of the following:
    _____ a. driving the Axis powers from North Africa
    _____ b. the Battle of Normandy
    _____ c. an invasion of Italy
    _____ d. Doolittle's raid
    _____ e. the drive across France
    _____ f. closing in on Germany from the east and the west

33. Four steps leading to American victory on the Pacific front included:
    _____ a. Doolittle's raid
    _____ b. the ground fighting of marines
    _____ c. naval victories in the Coral and Philippine seas
    _____ d. the land invasion of Japan
    _____ e. the bombing of Hiroshima

34. Five of the following the United States did to counter Soviet threats to free nations:
    _____ a. Korean conflict
    _____ b. the Bay of Pigs
    _____ c. NATO and SEATO
    _____ d. Marshall Plan
    _____ e. Sino-Soviet Pact
    _____ f. Vietnam

35. Communists successfully took over in all of the following countries *except*:
    _____ a. China
    _____ b. Cuba
    _____ c. Laos
    _____ d. the Philippines
    _____ e. North Korea
    _____ f. Vietnam

36.   Nixon sought to correct the ill-will over Vietnam through all of these policies *except:*

_____ a. the rehabilitation programs

_____ b. an honorable withdrawal of American troops

_____ c. an immediate withdrawal from Vietnam

_____ d. Vietnamization

Answer the following question (each answer, 4 points).

37.   What were the goals of the United States and the Soviet Union in the Cold War?

_____

_____

_____

_____

_____

Fill in the blank.

2.1 _____ means "made valid by approving."

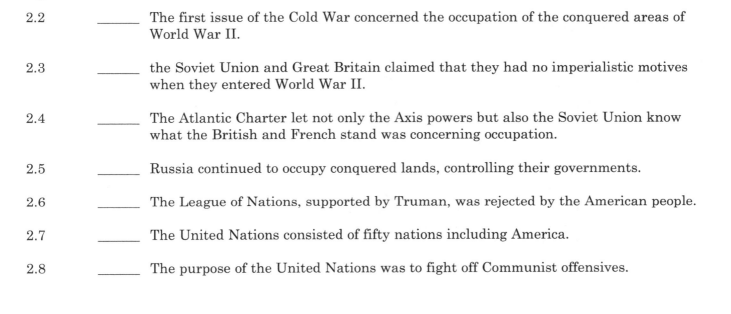 **True/False.**

2.2 _____ The first issue of the Cold War concerned the occupation of the conquered areas of World War II.

2.3 _____ the Soviet Union and Great Britain claimed that they had no imperialistic motives when they entered World War II.

2.4 _____ The Atlantic Charter let not only the Axis powers but also the Soviet Union know what the British and French stand was concerning occupation.

2.5 _____ Russia continued to occupy conquered lands, controlling their governments.

2.6 _____ The League of Nations, supported by Truman, was rejected by the American people.

2.7 _____ The United Nations consisted of fifty nations including America.

2.8 _____ The purpose of the United Nations was to fight off Communist offensives.

Choose the best answer.

2.9 How did the viewpoints of the United States and Great Britain differ from Soviet ideas concerning occupation and government in conquered lands of World War II? _____
   a. they wanted to equally divide the territory
   b. they wanted a larger share of the territory
   c. they didn't want any territory
   d. they wanted the Soviet Union to occupy the conquered land in Europe only

2.10 One of the reasons the United Nations was off to a better start than the League of Nations was because: _____
   a. the U.S. congress and people supported it.
   b. all the countries agreed to the policy of isolationism.
   c. Woodrow Wilson promoted it.
   d. they were preparing for the next World War.

Choose the best answer(s).

2.11   The nation that did not take part in the Potsdam meetings was: _____
    a.   the Soviet Union
    b.   France
    c.   Great Britain
    d.   the United States

2.12   Decisions of the Potsdam meetings included: _____ , _____ , _____ , _____
    a.   German disarmament
    b.   a cut-back of occupation troops
    c.   the development of German democratic government
    d.   the withdrawal of all Allied troops
    e.   the trial of Nazi leaders

2.13   A Soviet action that almost triggered another European conflict was: _____
    a.   Communist propaganda
    b.   Soviet criticism of a better society
    c.   the cutting back of wartime armed forces strength
    d.   the Potsdam meeting

2.14   NATO made possible: _____
    a.   Western Europe's economic recovery
    b.   Western Europe's control by the Soviet Union
    c.   the defense of Western Europe
    d.   United States imperialism in Europe

Match these items.

2.15   _____ Potsdam   a. the trial of former Nazi leaders

2.16   _____ Nuremberg   b. a meeting to determine future of occupied European nations

2.17   _____ Truman Doctrine   c. United States and British supply of necessities to Berlin

2.18   _____ Marshall Plan   d. aid to countries willing to adhere to the program

2.19   _____ Berlin Airlift   e. an organization for defense of Western Europe

2.20   _____ NATO   f. American support of countries opposed to Communism

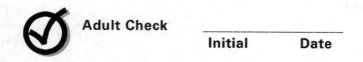

Adult Check   _____
                   Initial   **Date**

28

KOREAN CONFLICTS: THE COLD WAR BECOMES HOT

The problem of containing Communist aggression was by no means limited to Europe. Asia also had the problem of making a stand against the political movement of Communism that was threatening to infect the whole Pacific area. During the late 1940s and the early 1950s, the United Nations was faced with keeping peace in Asia. The Korean

CHIANG KAI-SHEK

War was the first war in which the United Nations played a military role. The war was a major challenge for the United Nations and tested the ability of this international body to keep peace in the world.

The Korean War began on June 25, 1950, when troops from Communist-ruled North Korea invaded South Korea at the urging of the Soviet Union. The United Nations called the invasion a violation of international peace and demanded that the Communists withdraw. When the Communists continued fighting, the United Nations asked its member nations to give military aid to South Korea. Sixteen United Nations countries sent troops and forty-one countries sent military equipment and supplies to South Korea. The United States sent more than 90 percent of the troops, military equipment, food, and other supplies to South Korea. China fought on the side of North Korea and the Soviet Union supplied the necessary military equipment to the North Koreans. The Korean War ended on July 27, 1953, when the United Nations and North Korea signed a truce to end the fighting. A permanent peace treaty, however, has never been signed.

Communist aggression in the Far East. In the late 1940s the Chinese Red army led by Mao Zedong continued to record victories on China's mainland over the Nationalist army headed by Chiang Kai-shek. In an effort to unite the country, the United States attempted to bring these two sides together for peace talks. In 1946 President Truman sent former General George C. Marshall to China as a mediator between the Chinese Communist Party and the Chinese Nationalist Party, or the **Kuomintang**. Having made some inroads at first, Marshall bitterly left China without achieving any lasting success. Marshall's departure was followed by even more intense fighting in China's civil war.

By December, 1949, because of numerous military blunders and poor management and morale, Chiang's Nationalist army was driven off China's mainland to the island of Formosa. Mao Zedong set up the People's Republic of China and established a Communist government. Additionally, much to the dismay of the United States, Mao began an immediate diplomatic relationship with the Soviet Union. Upon doing so, the Red Chinese began a relentless attack against the American presence and influence in Asia.

Although some people disagreed, the Communist victory in China was interpreted by many as a defeat to the United States in its international battle against Communism. China's revolution now posed a very serious challenge to the United States in the Far East. A confrontation would surely take place and the hostilities soon came to a head.

When China and the Soviet Union signed the Sino-Soviet Pact in February of 1950, most people in the United States believed that an international conspiracy was underway for a Communist takeover in Asia. The United States quickly responded by supporting France in its Indochina War against the Communist-backed forces of Ho Chi Minh. This support resulted in failure. The French eventually pulled out of the fighting because of their heavy losses of both men and money.

The United States faced its stiffest test since World War II in the Far East when in June of 1950 North Korean Communists swept down upon a poorly prepared South Korea. Although the United States was involved somewhat in Korean affairs following World War II, the expectation was that the situation would pass in time. Actually the situation did pass, but only temporarily.

In 1945 the Soviets had entered North Korea in their last effort to occupy as much land as possible at the end of World War II. The United States had already sent troops to South Korea under the leadership of General Douglas MacArthur. General MacArthur was present to accept the surrender of the Japanese. Initially, the tension mounted between the United States and the Soviet Union, but time had gradually eased the situation. Then, in compliance with a United Nations' request, the United States phased out their military assistance to South Korea. By January of 1950 the southern half of the Korean peninsula had been left on its own militarily. As commendations for making the proper decision continued to arrive in Washington and with assurances that the nation of Korea could live peaceably, the United States believed that the situation necessitated little further attention.

National Archives

General Douglas MacArthur

The North Korean attack of June 25, 1950, however, shattered the hope for peace in Korea. The United States preferred not to get involved in another war, especially in Asia, but that hope was also shattered. The North Korean army poured over the 38th parallel and promptly pushed the South Korean army to the southernmost part of the peninsula, just outside of the city of Pusan. The defensive line they established there was called the Pusan Perimeter. Talk of pushing the South Koreans right into the Sea of Japan (also called the East Sea) became a distinct possibility. Syngman Rhee, leader of the South Korean government, desperately pleaded with the United Nations and the United States for help.

President Truman responded to Rhee's request by immediately supplying air and sea support. However, it soon became evident that this aid would not be enough to hold off the Communist invaders. Thus, the United States was forced to send in ground forces under General Douglas MacArthur. The aid allowed the combined South Korean and American forces to hold at the Pusan perimeter. The U.N. denounced the communist aggression and asked its members to also send troops, and many did.

General MacArthur was named as the U.N. commander and quickly went into action. He was not going to fight a defensive war. On September 15, 1950, the United States army made a surprise amphibious landing at Inchon, just south of the 38th parallel and a few miles from Seoul, the Korean capital city. Cutting the forces of the North Koreans in half, the landing threw the Communists into disorganized retreat. By mid-autumn of 1950, the joint effort of the United States and the South Korean soldiers had driven the Communists right to the North Korean-Manchurian border. The United States soldiers began believing the rumors that they would be home to surprise their families for Christmas. Unfortunately, the United States army was the one who was surprised.

Contrary to what both President Truman and General MacArthur had predicted, Chinese "volunteers" (actually units of the Chinese Red Army) entered the war in October of 1950 on the side of the North Koreans. The tables had turned—both the United States and South Korea were pushed back by the Chinese Communists and the North Koreans. At that time the First Marine Division made its famous miraculous retreat from the Chosin Reservoir area on the China-North Korean border. In subzero weather and battling heavy snowstorms, the marines somehow eluded the Communist trap that had encircled them at the frozen Chosin. By January of 1951, however, the United States, South Korea and other United Nations groups had been forced to retreat below the 38th parallel once again.

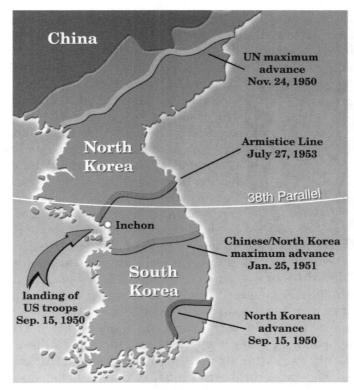

The Korean Conflict 1950-1953

Because of his defiance of President Truman's philosophy of containment in the Korean conflict, General Douglas MacArthur was relieved of his command in Korea on April 10, 1951. The general was opposed to allowing the stalemate in the war to continue. He suggested an offensive strategy that could have plunged the United States into a full-scale war with China, a conflict which not only President Truman but also many other military leaders definitely did not want.

When MacArthur returned to the United States, he received a hero's welcome from the people. MacArthur had many supporters who agreed with his idea of fighting an all-out war with the Communists and he said that we must win. The general eventually pleaded his cause with an emotional and spectacular speech before Congress. He explained his convictions against fighting a limited war by stating that there is no substitute for victory. MacArthur left his audience stirred by his eloquent performance and final remark, "Old soldiers never die, they just fade away." With all the pressure the MacArthur issue had brought about, President Truman still held the line on his containment policy in Korea and the defense of the Nationalist Chinese on the island of Formosa.

In October of 1951, peace negotiations began in Panmunjom, Korea. Fighting continued for almost two more years with little ground being gained past the 38th parallel on either side. Finally, in July of 1953, a permanent armistice was signed. The president of the United States, then Dwight D. Eisenhower, had stated in his election campaign that he would go to Korea to see what he could do to terminate the war. Many believed his influence did exactly that.

The police action, which the United Nations labeled their intervention in Korea, was one of the first major tests for the United Nations. The United States supported the major effort in the conflict and there was also enough international cooperation to cause a ray of optimism for future peacekeeping measures by the newly formed international body.

Peace negotiations. Among the world's leaders, a key contributor to the planning of world peace was the president of the United States. It was an awesome responsibility, but both Franklin D. Roosevelt and Harry S. Truman did commendable jobs as president during and at the end of World War II in working for a more peaceful future. Following Truman's term in office was a man quite capable of building on both Roosevelt's and Truman's efforts. Dwight D. Eisenhower was elected to the office of president in 1952.

Dwight D. Eisenhower

Eisenhower was an excellent choice for a nation that needed a strong leader who could deal with problems both at home and overseas. The respect Eisenhower received both nationally and internationally was sorely needed for the morale and the prestige of the United States. In 1952 the citizens of the United States not only had a deep fear of Communism, but they also had a concern about inflation, taxes, and federal spending, problems which still haunt the nation today. Conservative leadership was needed to check the expansion of a welfare state and Eisenhower provided that guidance.

Eisenhower's promise to go to Korea with the intention of bringing an end to the Far Eastern conflict certainly did not hurt his election campaign. Actually, the assumption generally was that if anyone could accomplish a peace settlement, Eisenhower could do it.

The former general had an appealing personality and a respected reputation. In addition to his military experience, Eisenhower was well educated in the important areas of economics and diplomacy. One of the major points of Eisenhower's campaign was a strong foreign policy. A young lawyer and senator from California, Richard M. Nixon, was selected as Eisenhower's running mate for Vice President. Richard M. Nixon was known to the people for his successful battles against Communism. Eisenhower and Nixon defeated their Democratic opponents, Adlai Stevenson of Illinois and Estes Kefauver of Tennessee.

Although a military man, Eisenhower sought to establish and to maintain peace. His intentions were honest and he had the ability to organize and to lead people toward what he considered achievable goals. To understand these traits, a look into Eisenhower's background will be helpful.

Dwight D. Eisenhower was born in Texas in 1890 and was reared in Abilene, Kansas. After graduating from Abilene High School in 1909, Eisenhower worked for two years and then entered West Point in 1911. He graduated from the military academy in 1915 and began a career in the army that would eventually lead him to the highest military rank, a five-star general of the army.

Eisenhower was able to observe the attempt at negotiations for peace following World War I. He never served in combat during World War I; however, he did spend time traveling abroad observing the aftermath of the war. He realized that the international scene was insecure and that the United States needed to remain strong militarily in order to influence peace. The League of Nations and other efforts to negotiate peace had little effect on those nations with ambitious desires. With other nations weakly prepared militarily, the aggressors had little deterrent to prevent them from conquering nation after nation.

Eisenhower was promoted from colonel to brigadier general in 1941, a few months before the U.S. entered World War II. In 1942 he supervised the Allied operations in North Africa against the Germans. He proved to be a very skilled diplomat, getting all the various Allied commanders to work together during a complex invasion. After leading other successful offensives against the Germans, Eisenhower was appointed as Commander of the Allied Forces in Europe. He was, therefore, in command of the crucially important invasion of Normandy, France on June 6, 1944.

Following World War II, Eisenhower served as Army Chief of Staff until he retired from military service in 1948 to become president of Columbia University for two years. In 1950 Eisenhower agreed to aid in the setting up of the North Atlantic Treaty Organization (NATO) in an effort to halt Communist growth in Europe. His efforts kept the problem-riddled European scene from exploding into combat many times. The NATO program and other projects in which Eisenhower negotiated saved lives both in the United States and in Europe. He retired from NATO to run for president.

During the two terms of Eisenhower's administration, an emphasis was always on military preparation. When Congress pressed for a tax cut, Eisenhower wisely held off until it could be done without hurting the nation's defense. Eisenhower, keenly aware of the military buildups of Communist Russia and Communist China, had no intention of losing the Cold War. The Communist strategy of taking nations over either peaceably or by force had little opportunity to succeed under Eisenhower. His strong stand for a militarily prepared nation was an excellent method of negotiating for peace.

Not only was Eisenhower effective in peace negotiations outside the nation, but he also dealt with domestic problems in a firm manner. President Eisenhower supported the National Defense Education Act (NDEA) in 1958. This act provided federal money for studies in mathematics and science fields along with teacher training, an act Eisenhower believed was necessary for the improvement of this nation's future security.

Eisenhower knew that political and economic relations with foreign countries could be developed into healthy friendships that would insure peaceful relationships. Trade was developed with other nations and foreign aid was strongly supported by Eisenhower. Eisenhower believed that financial help for European countries was needed to help them recover from the Second World War. Many nations were given foreign aid as a deterrent to Communism. Thus, in a sense, United States government was paying countries not to join with, or to be overly friendly with, Communist nations.

Eisenhower also had his problems, however. The recession of 1957 and its widespread unemployment hurt his popular image. Also, some people thought that Eisenhower did not back his strong words against Communism in Asia and did not strongly support the Nationalist Chinese on the island of Formosa. However, Eisenhower's administration of eight years maintained stability in turbulent times.

Choose the best answer(s).

2.21   What four concerns did the United States have when Eisenhower took office?

_____ a. Communism

_____ b. corporation control

_____ c. inflation

_____ d. taxes

_____ e. federal spending

2.22   One factor that made Eisenhower a good choice for president was:

_____ a. a lack of military experience

_____ b. his experience in diplomatic relations

_____ c. a fervor for war

_____ d. a lack of strength

2.23   A factor of Eisenhower's foreign policy included:

_____ a. developing friendships with foreign countries

_____ b. standing behind the League of Nations

_____ c. helping foreign nations become communist

_____ d. aiding the setting up of NDEA

True/False.

2.24 _____ After winning the Chinese civil war, Kai-shek set up the People's Republic of China.

2.25 _____ The Sino-Soviet Pact joined China and the Soviet Union in a treaty.

2.26 _____ France failed in its attempts to drive the Communists from Indochina.

2.27 _____ After Rhee's Chinese volunteers entered the Korean conflict, the South Koreans were again pushed below the 38th parallel.

2.28 _____ The Marine retreat from the Chosin Reservoir area was accomplished easily.

2.29 _____ MacArthur was opposed to Truman's policy of containment in Korea.

Match the following.

2.30 _____ Mao Zedong   a. Chinese Nationalist leader

2.31 _____ Chiang Kai-shek   b. the Communist leader in Indochina War

2.32 _____ Marshall   c. a United States mediator in Chinese civil war

2.33 _____ Ho Chi Minh   d. the United States commander in Korean conflict

2.34 _____ Syngman Rhee   e. the leader of South Korean government

2.35 _____ Chinese "volunteers" f. allies of North Korean Communists

2.36 _____ MacArthur   g. opposed all-out United States war with China

2.37 _____ Truman   h. Chinese Red army leader

Match these items.

2.38 _____ Adlai Stevenson   a. Eisenhower's opponent during the election of 1952

2.39 _____ Dwight D. Eisenhower   b. Nationalist Chinese Republic

2.40 _____ Richard Nixon   c. Adlai Stevenson's running mate

2.41 _____ NDEA   d. West Point graduate, president of the United States

2.42 _____ Estes Kefauver   e. Eisenhower's vice president

2.43 _____ Formosa   f. provided money for studies in math and science

Adult Check _____
                    Initial   **Date**

 Review the material in this section in preparation for the Self Test. This Self Test will check your mastery of this particular section as well as your knowledge of the previous sections.

SELF TEST 2

Match these items (each answer, 2 points).

2.01 _____ Churchill

2.02 _____ MacArthur

2.03 _____ Mao Zedong

2.04 _____ Chiang Kai-shek

2.05 _____ Truman

2.06 _____ Eisenhower

2.07 _____ Doolittle

2.08 _____ Mussolini

2.09 _____ Hitler

2.010 _____ Marshall

a. Allied commander in the Far East

b. Italian dictator in World War II

c. German dictator during World War II

d. British Prime Minister

e. commander of Allied forces in World War II

f. leader of the Chinese Red army

g. president at the end of World War II

h. created a plan of financial aid to countries

i. led the United States attack on Tokyo

j. leader of Chinese Nationalists

Match each item with its significance (each answer, 2 points).

2.011 _____ Battle of Normandy

2.012 _____ Pusan Perimeter

2.013 _____ Hiroshima and Nagasaki

2.014 _____ Pearl Harbor

2.015 _____ Atlantic Charter

2.016 _____ Marshall Plan

2.017 _____ Sino-Soviet Pact

2.018 _____ United Nations

2.019 _____ NATO

a. Chinese and Soviet agreement

b. brought the United States into WWII

c. line that held against the North Korean invasion

d. invasion of France

e. security and defense against Communism

f. atomic bombs

g. to rebuild Europe

h. U.S. and Britain would not seek territorial gain

i. world organization to overcome differences

True/False (each answer, 1 point).

2.020 _____ The Allied powers were Italy, Germany, and Japan.

2.021 _____ The military build-ups of Hitler and Mussolini gave them the advantage over nearby smaller countries.

2.022 _____ Although the United States and Great Britain sought no power over occupied countries after World War II, the Soviet Union did.

2.023   _____ The United Nations had a more successful start than the League of Nations.

2.024   _____ The Potsdam meeting resulted in American support of countries opposed to Communism.

2.025   _____ When the Soviet Union cut off western supply routes to Berlin, the United States and Great Britain responded with the Berlin Airlift.

2.026   _____ The trials of Nuremberg gave many Nazi leaders the death sentence.

2.027   _____ The Korean conflict staged Americans and North Koreans against the Chinese and South Koreans.

2.028   _____ MacArthur was opposed to Truman's policy of containment in Korea.

2.029   _____ After driving the Chinese Nationalists to Formosa, Chiang Kai-shek set up the People's Republic of China.

Choose the best answer(s) (each answer, 2 points).

2.030   An Axis victory in World War II was the:
- _____ a. driving of Germans from North Africa.
- _____ b. invasion of Normandy.
- _____ c. Doolittle's raid.
- _____ d. Battle of Guadalcanal.
- _____ e. attack on Pearl Harbor.

2.031   In the early 1940s the United States determined to prove to the world that her motives for entering World War II were:
- _____ a. imperialistic.
- _____ b. to attack the Soviet Union.
- _____ c. to re-establish peace in the world.
- _____ d. to gain new possessions.

2.032   Indicate four counteractions the United States and Britain took in response to Communist expansion in Europe:
- _____ a. Truman Doctrine
- _____ b. the Marshall Plan
- _____ c. the Berlin Airlift
- _____ d. the Nuremberg meetings
- _____ e. NATO

2.033   A political action taken by Mao Zedong was the:
- _____ a. establishment of the People's Republic of China.
- _____ b. answering of Rhee's pleas for help.
- _____ c. linking of China with Germany in the Sino-German Pact.
- _____ d. authorization of the Koreans to join in the Korean conflict.
- _____ e. driving of Chinese Nationalists to Vietnam.

2.034   One part of Eisenhower's foreign policy was:
- _____ a. helping foreign nations recover from war.
- _____ b. financial aid to the Soviet Union.
- _____ c. aid in developing Sino-Soviet Pact.
- _____ d. support of Sino-Soviet Pact.

2.035   The United States and British viewpoints concerning Allied occupation and government in
conquered World War II lands differed from Soviet policies because:

_____ a. they didn't want any territory.
_____ b. they wanted to equally divide the territory.
_____ c. they wanted a larger share of the territory.
_____ d. they wanted the Soviet Union to occupy the conquered land in Europe only.

Fill in the blanks (each answer, 3 points).

2.036   NATO was organized to halt the growth of _____ in Europe.

2.037   MacArthur was relieved of his command in the Korean conflict because he defied President

_____ .

Score
Adult Check

_____

_____
Initial   Date

III. VIETNAM CONFLICT

The United States had become aware of the determination of the Communists to stand firmly in their Cold War position against free-world nations. By putting down uprisings in the 1950s in East Germany and Hungary with speed and cruelty, the Communists demonstrated their commitment not to give up the land they had occupied since World War II.

In this section you will study American reaction to the Soviet aggression. To counteract the Soviet advance, the United States had to execute timely and firm action—action that would command Russian respect. In an attempt to counter the Communists, therefore, the United States came to the military aid of South Vietnam. During the early years of the war in the 1950s, the United States sent military advisors to assist the government and the army of South Vietnam. As the Communists advanced the war, however, the United States sent military aid in the form of supplies and troops to help the people of South Vietnam. Although the United States never officially declared war, more than five hundred thousand United States military men were involved in the war by February of 1969.

SECTION OBJECTIVES

Review these objectives. When you have completed this section, you should be able to:

8. List the steps taken by President Kennedy in the United States' increased resistance to communist world infiltration:

    8.1 Examine the Cuban and Berlin crisis under Kennedy's administration.

    8.2 Explain the United States' involvement in the Vietnamese War.

9. Describe President Nixon's plan for withdrawal from Vietnam.

10. Describe the effects of the Vietnamese War upon United States servicemen and civilians.

VOCABULARY

Study these words to enhance your learning success in this section.

fiasco	A complete or humiliating failure
garrison	A place where military force is stationed for defense
infiltration	Penetration for the purpose of subversive activity
pacifist	One who opposes military ideals, war or military preparedness and instead seeks settlement of disputes by arbitration
rehabilitation	The act of restoring to a state of health and useful activity through training, therapy, and guidance
Vietnamization	The gradual transfer of fighting in Vietnam from United States soldiers to South Vietnamese troops

VIETNAM: FIGHTING COMMUNISM IN SOUTHEAST ASIA

COMMUNISM IN SOUTHEAST ASIA

In the late 1950s the Soviets shocked the Western world when they launched their first earth-orbiting satellite on October 4, 1957. The initial *Sputnik* was soon followed by the launching of additional satellites, bringing an uncomfortable feeling to the citizens of the United States. Fearing the Soviets could use their space advantage in a military way, the public clamored for increased American involvement to match the Soviet space program which had showered the Soviets with a great amount of international prestige.

Considering both the danger of the Soviet Union's growing influence in space and its ambitious desire to take over more lands on earth, the United States became determined to meet the Soviet challenge. When the United States successfully launched its first satellite, the space race was underway between the United States and the Soviet Union with each nation using its modern technology in an attempt to maintain an edge on the other.

Meanwhile, the Cold War struggle continued as both the Soviet Union and the United States intensified their drive to influence neutral nations throughout the world. Prime targets included such nations as India, Pakistan, Burma, Indonesia, countries in Africa, and Asia, as well as some Arab countries. Often, however, these nations had no desire to choose either Communism or democracy; they merely wanted to conduct their own affairs, surviving as best they could.

Prewar activities. To resist Communist expansion in Asia, the Southeast Asia Treaty Organization (SEATO)–an organization similar to NATO–was formed. SEATO included the nations of Great Britain, Australia, France, Pakistan, New Zealand, Thailand, the Philippines, and the United States. The United States was determined to stand behind the treaty and to help it become effective internationally.

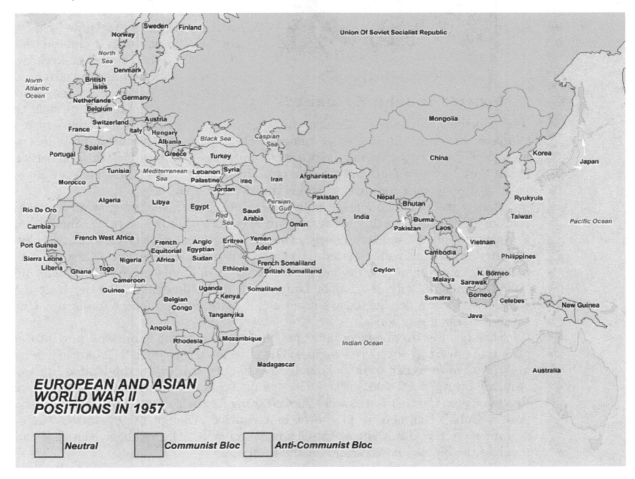

EUROPEAN AND ASIAN WORLD WAR II POSITIONS IN 1957

Neutral   Communist Bloc   Anti-Communist Bloc

The United States was committed to a role of at least containing Communism in the world. The desire to liberate countries from the Soviet domination was strong within the hearts of many people in the United States. Unfortunately, delivering people and nations from the Iron Curtain in Europe and the Bamboo Curtain in Asia was an extremely difficult task. Both the United States and the Soviet Union were involved in intense competition, but neither country wanted to risk an all-out war. Nevertheless, the challenges and confrontations steadily increased with a clear understanding of the possible costs involved.

However, when the Soviet Communist leader Joseph Stalin died, the Soviets eased some of their hard-line stands. The new leaders became somewhat more open to international diplomacy and sensitivity. Although confrontations were still prevalent, Soviet policy demonstrated a shift in mood and tactics.

Organizations such as NATO and SEATO took an effective stand against Communism in Europe and Asia, but Soviet **infiltration** continued reaching throughout the Middle East, Latin America, and Africa. The claws of the Russian Bear were positioned for takeover. Once again, the United States took the defensive and offered assistance in terms of military aid, advice, trade, foreign aid, and overall availability. The extent of these preventive measures by the United States in backing threatened nations who wished to be self-governing can never be accurately estimated.

National Archives

President John F. Kennedy

John F. Kennedy's role. Although President Eisenhower's administration was reputed to be stable and generally peaceful, there was a great deal of turmoil beneath the calm surface. As John F. Kennedy assumed the responsibilities of the Presidency, the areas of suppressed trouble began to erupt. Following the legendary and fatherly image of President Eisenhower was not an easy task. Nevertheless, the youthful ex-senator from Massachusetts gave the United States a positive and optimistic outlook as it entered the 1960s.

To continue the popular and relatively successful foreign policy inherited from Eisenhower, President Kennedy initiated the Peace Corps on March 1, 1961. The main purpose of this program was to send volunteers to foreign countries with United States technology, methods and "Yankee" ingenuity. By doing so, underdeveloped countries would be able to enjoy a better lifestyle with improvements in medical and sanitary techniques. The idea and early efforts of the Peace Corps were to share the abundance of the United States. These efforts were accepted in a positive way by most countries to which they were offered.

Some aspects of the foreign policy inherited from Eisenhower were not good. Unstable relationships with South American countries, for example, were strained at many levels. Foreign aid, often used improperly from the American point of view, at times seemed to be resented rather than appreciated. The Cuban situation was nearly at the explosion point. The Cuban Revolution had resulted in the dictatorship of Fidel Castro in 1959, who quickly established friendship with the Soviet Union and made his disdain for the United States very clear. The Cuban premier also served as an agitator attempting to disrupt United States-Latin American relations.

Shortly after Kennedy became president, an invasion plan was put into action in an attempt to overthrow Castro's regime. The invasion troops—exiled Cuban soldiers who desperately wanted to return to their homeland—had been trained by the United States. The attack occurred on April 17, 1961 at the Cienaga de Zapata swamps of Las Villas Province (Bay of Pigs) in Cuba. Castro's forces were far too strong for the gallant exiles and the anticipated support of Cuba's common people never materialized. Though the operation was planned and organized by the U.S. Central Intelligence Agency (CIA), President Kennedy had to assume much of the blame and criticism for the **fiasco.**

Besides an unstable relationship with Latin America and the problems of a divided Europe, President Kennedy inherited an additional situation that would become far more widespread and controversial than the Cuban situation had been. Asia in general—and Southeast Asia in particular—had been in deep turmoil since the end of World War II. The takeover of China by the Communists in 1949 only intensified the growing unrest. When the French were finally driven out of Indochina in 1954, the situation appeared to improve with the end of Western colonialism. However, unresolved hostilities in the Southeast Asian countries, especially Vietnam, erupted in civil war.

The struggles within these countries were mainly between the democratic forces and the Communist forces. By the early sixties, the Communist guerrilla forces in North Vietnam led by Ho Chi Minh were inching steadily closer to a takeover of the South Vietnamese government headed by Ngo Dinh Diem. The poorly motivated Vietnamese people of the south were no match either for the ruthless and resourceful Vietcong (southern communists) or for the regular soldiers of the north.

In an effort to help the struggling republic of South Vietnam, Kennedy offered even more military aid than had Eisenhower's administration. In addition, Kennedy sent military advisors to help train the South Vietnamese troops. From the American point of view, the situation continued to deteriorate and there never seemed to be a sufficient number of United States advisors or military equipment. Disaster struck when the Kennedy-backed Diem was assassinated by a group of South Vietnamese Army generals. President Kennedy was beginning to perceive, as Eisenhower had, that the situation was far more intense than had been anticipated by his administration forecasts.

At the same time the Communists were also presenting a challenge in Germany. To stop the flow of thousands of East German refugees into West Germany, the Soviets began the construction of a wall between East Berlin and West Berlin in August of 1961. Furious at the number of German people who streamed across the border to escape their government, the Communists interpreted this action as a mounting disgrace taking place before an international audience. The mass exodus had at one point reached a thousand per day. By stopping the flow of refugees, the Soviets could save face. The East Germans, unfortunately, had little choice.

Building of the Berlin Wall

For a short time both Soviet and United States military equipment was positioned on opposite sides of the wall. Furthermore, extra United States army, navy, and air force units were mobilized in the event of hostilities. Eventually, the crisis passed and East Germany remained segregated while West Germany became a separate republic. Because of the bitterness remaining from World War II and the horrible price that the Soviet Union paid in lives to capture Berlin during the war, the stalemate over the divided city and country was generally accepted.

Another serious challenge to the United States was the Cuban missile crisis. On October 22, 1962, President Kennedy revealed to the United States public that Soviet Premier Nikita Khrushchev and Cuban Dictator Fidel Castro had made an agreement to set up missiles in Cuba. The resulting danger to America's defense was frightening.

Kennedy immediately called for a Cuban blockade that would prevent Cuba from receiving military equipment until an agreement could be reached between the two countries.

As tension mounted, Kennedy and Khrushchev wrestled with the difficult decisions of what actions to risk. A restless world anxiously awaited the outcome, well aware that nations were being drawn closer to the brink of World War. Finally, on November 2, 1962, a relieved Kennedy informed the country that the crisis had ended in reconciliation. The Soviets agreed to dismantle their missiles in exchange for a pledge from the United States not to invade Cuba.

President Kennedy had made it quite clear to the Soviet Union and to international Communism that the United States would stand behind its commitment to halt Communist advances around the world. Challenges would inevitably continue; but the lessons of Korea, Berlin, and Cuba demonstrated to the world that the United States would take a stand even if all the details did not work out well. Although John Kennedy did not live to see the results of all his decisions, the people of the United States are well aware of the firm but cautious inroads he made in pursuing this nation's defense.

National Archives

President Lyndon B. Johnson

Lyndon B. Johnson's role. Following the commitment of President Eisenhower to stand behind the South Vietnamese government and President Kennedy's move to send United States soldiers as advisors, the United States found itself becoming more involved in the Vietnamese War.

When Vice President Lyndon Johnson became president following the assassination of John F. Kennedy, he firmly believed in following the policies of Kennedy's administration, particularly those policies concerning foreign affairs. He vowed to take strong action in Southeast Asia, if necessary, to keep Communism from advancing in the Pacific area. Like Kennedy and Eisenhower, President Johnson assumed that military aid and advisors were all that would be necessary to help the South Vietnamese resist the North Vietnamese. The United States apparently underestimated the vast system of well organized and well supported Vietcong guerrillas firmly entrenched in the South and the lack of military initiative on the part of the South Vietnamese. Therefore, the willingness of the United States to train the unskilled South Vietnamese soldiers gradually drew the United States into a more active role and into eventual combat. By 1964 over twenty thousand United States troops were in Vietnam, a number that was soon multiplied many times.

The final step in this nation's commitment to war occurred in August of 1964 when President Johnson asked Congress to pass a resolution concerning the Southeast Asian conflict. Congress responded by accepting the Gulf of Tonkin resolution. United States ships had recently experienced an attack by the North Vietnamese in the Gulf of Tonkin. By this resolution the president was given authority to retaliate militarily not only for this but also for other incidents. The resolution marked the beginning of an arms and the mobilization of troops that Presidents Eisenhower and Kennedy had probably not anticipated. However, President Johnson was intent on proving to the Communists that he would stand firmly against a Communist takeover of Southeast Asia.

Interestingly enough, Lyndon Johnson's election campaign in 1964 was based heavily on the premise of not escalating the fighting in Vietnam. The Republican candidate, Barry Goldwater, accused the Democrats of supporting a no-win policy in Vietnam. One of the main reasons for the Democratic victory appeared to be that the people of the United States believed Johnson would keep them out of a war and that Goldwater probably would not.

By early 1965, however, the war escalated rapidly. Following several incidents in which United States advisors were killed, Johnson authorized the bombing of a North Vietnamese port. The president had been advised that this type of action would bring a quick settlement with Ho Chi Minh to end the war. Instead, as time passed and Ho Chi Minh resisted, the bombing became even more intense and widespread. Rather than destroying the morale of the North Vietnamese, the bombing of Hanoi and other areas seemed to strengthen their fighting spirit. Consequently, the strategic effect of halting infiltration into South Vietnam was minimal. As American troops became increasingly more frustrated because they could not end the war quickly with the bombing, the North Vietnamese and Vietcong in South Vietnam dug in and prepared for a long, intense conflict.

The commander in charge of the United States forces in South Vietnam was General William Westmoreland. American personnel grew to one hundred twenty-five thousand in 1965, two hundred thousand in 1966 and over five hundred thousand by 1967. In spite of this build-up, the enemy still remained extremely elusive. The bombings in North Vietnam did little to check the infiltration of supplies and men to South Vietnam. As soon as United States troops left a conquered area, the Vietcong returned. The same villages could be captured and recaptured a number of times. Land could not be taken and then fortified; the terrain of rice paddies, swamps, and various fields made a **garrison** situation quite impossible.

Vietnam Protests

Vietnamese War, 1969
■ U.S. Military Bases

A dissatisfied and insecure mood began to surface in the United States causing pacifist protests to insist on an end to our country's involvement in Vietnam. Their concern seemed to be about the right of the United States to intervene militarily in the Vietnamese War. The drain on the United States economy was another complaint of the American people. The production of war materials increased; but inflation, higher taxes, and the devaluation of the American dollar on the international monetary market all had negative effects on the nation's financial status. The price the United States had to pay for the foreign war was growing far out of the limits predicted.

On the other hand, some people believed that an all-out war was the only answer for the United States and that all those who gave their lives would have died in vain if an absolute victory was not achieved. Therefore, the divisiveness among citizens and their representatives intensified daily.

The belief that taking a stand against Communism in Vietnam would ultimately prevent the Communists from getting to this country's borders, homes, and families, held some validity in the early years of the conflict. Eventually, however, many people came to believe that fighting near their borders and for their homes and country was extremely different from fighting for the Vietnamese people, who were seemingly indifferent to defending their own interests.

Paradoxically, the role of the United States serviceman in Vietnam was not that of a hero. Unless he volunteered for extra duty, a military man was only required to serve one year in Vietnam. Once that year was over, he completed his military obligations elsewhere.

Soldiers in Vietnam

Even when American victories did come they received little credit. Names of unpronounceable towns and cities in Vietnam were meaningless to many soldiers as well as to civilians. Da Nang, Khe Sanh, and Saigon were scenes of fierce battles in which many American lives were lost. Over thirty thousand United States servicemen gave their lives in these strange-sounding places, with thousands more wounded or missing in action.

The frustrating situation in Southeast Asia and the rising resentment at home became too great for many of our servicemen to handle. To escape the realities of the war and its consequences, many resorted to drugs. This problem did not remain in Vietnam, however, and some American GI's brought their drug addictions home with them, creating one of this country's most difficult **rehabilitation** assignments. In addition, the drug culture soon spread throughout this nation's high schools, heavily influencing and tempting thousands of students in the 1970s.

Before time for reelection in 1968, President Johnson had reevaluated his political future. In ill health and under severe pressure created by the war in Vietnam, Johnson decided against running for reelection.

Match these items.

3.1 _____ garrison

3.2 _____ infiltration

3.3 _____ rehabilitation

3.4 _____ fiasco

a. A complete or humiliating failure

b. A place where military force is stationed for defense

c. The act of restoring to a state of health and useful activity through training, therapy

d. Penetration for the purpose of subversive activity

Match these items.

3.5 _____ Castro

3.6 _____ Kennedy

3.7 _____ Ho Chi Minh

3.8 _____ Ngo Dinh Diem

3.9 _____ Khrushchev

a. Cuban dictator

b. head of the South Vietnamese government

c. successor to Dwight D. Eisenhower

d. Soviet premier

e. headed Communists in North Vietnam

True/False.

3.10 _____ The Soviet satellite *Sputnik* began the space race.

3.11 _____ SEATO, like NATO, was formed to resist Communist advances in Europe.

3.12 _____ Eisenhower's Peace Corps was successful in helping under-developed countries raise their living standards.

3.13 _____ The Central Intelligence Agency backed the Bay of Pigs invasion of Castro's Cuba.

3.14 _____ Kennedy's firm but cautious action in the Cuban missile crisis resulted in the disassembling of Soviet missiles sites.

3.15 _____ The Vietnam conflict arose between the democratic and republican forces in Vietnam.

Answer the following question.

3.16   How did the Peace Corps put the Biblical admonition, (Luke 12:48) "to whom much is given, much is expected," into action?

_____

_____

_____

_____

_____

✓ **Adult Check**   _____

                                     Initial   **Date**

Choose the best answer(s).

3.17   Three steps leading to American involvement in Vietnam were:
_____ a. the Gulf of Tonkin resolution
_____ b. military advisors sent by Kennedy
_____ c. American involvement on Formosa
_____ d. commitment of support by Eisenhower

3.18   What three things did President Johnson hope the bombing of North Vietnam would accomplish?
_____ a. settling the war quickly
_____ b. destroying North Vietnam morale
_____ c. halting North Vietnamese infiltration
_____ d. furthering the cause of the Vietcong

3.19   Three problems confronting United States servicemen in Vietnam included:
_____ a. frustrating situation in Southeast Asia
_____ b. rising resentment at home to the war in Vietnam
_____ c. increasing participation by friendly nations
_____ d. increasing drug addiction and alcoholism

Match these items.

3.20   _____ Westmoreland   a. resolution giving President Johnson authority to retaliate militarily in the Vietnam War

3.21   _____ Gulf of Tonkin   b. allies of North Vietnam

3.22   _____ Vietcong   c. accused Democrats of a no-win policy in Vietnam

3.23   _____ Kennedy   d. commander of American forces in Vietnam

3.24   _____ Goldwater   e. president who sent soldiers to South Vietnam as advisors

Fill in the blanks.

3.25   Johnson backed the war in Vietnam to show he would stand firmly in his intentions of

preventing a _____ takeover of Southeast _____ .

Answer the following question.

3.26   What does the Bible teach in Romans 13:1-7 (and other passages) concerning the backing of
governmental leaders, even when we do not agree with their policies?

_____

_____

_____

_____

_____

✓ **Adult Check**   _____

                      Initial   Date

WITHDRAWAL BY THE UNITED STATES

National Archives

President Richard M. Nixon

By 1968 many Americans had become divided over the Vietnam conflict and, more particularly, over the involvement of the United States in that conflict. In the spring of that year, President Johnson announced his decision not to run for reelection. Richard M. Nixon was elected to succeed Johnson. During his administration the war in Vietnam was brought to an end and United States troops stationed in Vietnam were withdrawn.

In this section you will study how this country "wound down" the war. A cease-fire was signed in January, 1973, thus ending American involvement in the war. Officially, the conflict ended on April 30, 1975, when South Vietnam surrendered to the Communists of North Vietnam.

Nixon's withdrawal policy. Richard M. Nixon, the new chief executive, had served as vice president to President Dwight D. Eisenhower for eight years. The Nixon administration inherited many difficulties and challenging situations from the previous administration. The war in Vietnam was certainly Nixon's major challenge. Another serious challenge was the inflation affecting the country's economy.

47

When President Nixon announced that 25,000 American servicemen would be withdrawn from Vietnam by the end of 1969, he executed the first step in his **Vietnamization** program. He specifically pointed out that these troops would be replaced by South Vietnamese soldiers. American leaders hoped that such a move would show North Vietnam how serious they were about the peace talks being held in Paris. Secretary of State Henry Kissinger believed that the move would instill confidence in the South Vietnamese and would also relieve some of the pressure at home from those demanding an immediate withdrawal. In the face of demonstrations and growing opposition by **pacifists**, including some politicians, President Nixon remained firm in his stand for an honorable withdrawal through the Vietnamization of the war.

The peace talks being held in Paris were serious efforts for peace and President Nixon was steadfast in his belief that the war in Vietnam was coming to an end. He believed that the winding down of hostilities would surely result from his plan to replace American troops with South Vietnamese soldiers. Step by step Nixon continued withdrawal of United States military forces from Vietnam. Although many believed the South Vietnamese did not have the strength and determination to resist the Vietcong and the North Vietnamese, the plan did gain international respect and began to calm the growing antagonism within the United States toward the Vietnam War.

Social unrest and moral problems. With the prospect of half a million servicemen returning home becoming a reality, the United States had a further challenge: the problem of helping those young men return to society in a purposeful way. The widespread problems of drug addiction and alcoholism among the soldiers in Southeast Asia called for intense government rehabilitation programs. Immorality and its accompanying diseases also presented serious problems. Although the government carried out rehabilitative and preventive programs, it did not sufficiently terminate the problems. A great increase in the use of drugs and in open immorality among the nation's teenagers, for example, was soon evident throughout the United States.

Psychologically, the returning servicemen often were shattered emotionally. Besides being repeatedly exposed to the threat of death and bloodshed, the war had caused many of these young men to question whether all the efforts of training, fighting, and loss of life had even been worthwhile. Some servicemen returned to find broken homes. Other families were faced with the adjustment to life without their loved ones who were either lost or missing in action.

Peace and defeat. The signing of a peace treaty by North Vietnam, the Vietcong, South Vietnam, and the United States occurred in Paris on January 27, 1973. The United States agreed to leave Vietnam within a sixty-day period. Free elections were to follow in South Vietnam, establishing a new government. After the final American pullout, however, the South Vietnamese military proved to be no match for their northern enemies. By 1975 not only did South Vietnam fall to the Communists, but so did Laos and Cambodia.

Vietnam War Memorial

True/False.

3.27 _____ The concept of Vietnamization gave international respect to the pullout of American troops from Vietnam.

3.28 _____ A peace treaty was signed in Paris by North Vietnam, the Vietcong, South Vietnam, and the United States on January 27, 1973.

3.29 _____ The United States agreed to leave Vietnam within six months.

3.30 _____ By 1975, South Vietnam, Laos, and Cambodia had fallen to the Communists.

Fill in the blanks.

3.31 One who opposes military ideals, war, or military preparedness and instead seeks settlement of disputes by arbitration is called _____ .

3.32 President Lyndon B. Johnson decided _____ for reelection in 1968.

3.33 The transfer of the fighting to the South Vietnamese by President Nixon was known as _____ .

3.34 United States Secretary of State under President Nixon was _____ .

3.35 Peace talks with the North Vietnamese were held in _____ .

Choose the best answer(s).

3.36 Nixon's policy of troop withdrawal from Vietnam was designed to be: _____ , _____
   a. slow
   b. honorable
   c. quick and immediate
   d. in opposition to the peace talks

3.37 American leaders hoped that Nixon's Vietnamization program would have the following results: _____ , _____ , _____
   a. show North Vietnam that the United States was serious about the Paris peace talks
   b. show confidence in the South Vietnamese forces
   c. lower inflation in the United States
   d. relieve the pressure of discontent at home

Adult Check _____
   Initial   Date

Before you take this last Self Test, you may want to do one or more of these self checks.

   1. _____ Read the objectives. Determine if you can do them.
   2. _____ Restudy the material related to any objectives that you cannot do.
   3. _____ Use the SQ3R study procedure to review the material:
      a. **S**can the sections.
      b. **Q**uestion yourself again (review the questions you wrote initially).
      c. **R**ead to answer your questions.
      d. **R**ecite the answers to yourself.
      e. **R**eview areas you didn't understand.
   4. _____ Review all activities and Self Tests, writing a correct answer for each wrong answer.

SELF TEST 3

Match these items (each answer, 2 points).

3.01	_____ Hitler	a.	an advisor to Nixon on foreign affairs
3.02	_____ Mussolini	b.	the Italian dictator during World War II
3.03	_____ Eisenhower	c.	the leader of the Chinese Red Army
3.04	_____ Churchill	d.	British prime minister during World War II
3.05	_____ MacArthur	e.	the Cuban dictator following Cuban Revolution
3.06	_____ Doolittle	f.	the leader of Communist forces in Indochina and North Vietnam
3.07	_____ Mao Zedong	g.	a German dictator during World War II
3.08	_____ Chiang Kai-shek	h.	the commander of United States in Pacific front, World War II
3.09	_____ Marshall	i.	he created financial aid program for European countries
3.010	_____ Castro	j.	a leader of Chinese Nationalist army
3.011	_____ Kissinger	k.	led United States bombing attack on Tokyo
3.012	_____ Khrushchev	l.	the commander of Allied forces on the European front during World War II
3.013	_____ Ho Chi Minh	m.	Soviet premier during the Cuban missile crisis
3.014	_____ Ngo Dinh Diem	n.	head of South Vietnam government

Match the following (each answer, 2 points).

3.015	_____ Battle of Normandy	a.	got the U.S. into World War II
3.016	_____ Pearl Harbor	b.	defense against Communism in Europe
3.017	_____ Hiroshima	c.	brought Japan defeat
3.018	_____ Gulf of Tonkin Resolution	d.	defense against Communism in Asia
3.019	_____ Vietnamization	e.	withdrawal from Vietnam
3.020	_____ United Nations	f.	between West and East to influence neutral nations
3.021	_____ NATO	g.	began battle for France
3.022	_____ SEATO	h.	settle world problems peacefully
3.023	_____ Cold War	i.	military involvement in Vietnam

True/False (each answer, 1 point).

3.024 _____ The military build-up of Germany and Italy set the stage for World War II.

3.025 _____ The German attack on Pearl Harbor brought the United States into World War II.

3.026 _____ The United States and Great Britain sought no power over in conquered lands after World War II.

3.027 _____ While Truman maintained a policy of containment in Korea, MacArthur sought an all-out war for victory.

3.028 _____ Kennedy's Peace Corps tried to develop better lifestyles in backward nations.

3.029 _____ Kennedy's cautious but firm treatment of the Cuban missile crisis resulted in the disassembling of Soviet missiles sites.

3.030 _____ The Potsdam meetings determined the future of occupied European nations following World War II.

3.031 _____ The Soviet satellite *Sputnik* started the space race between the United States and the Soviet Union.

Choose the best answer (each answer, 2 points).

3.032 The United States' counteraction to Communistic infiltration in Europe was: _____ .
   a. involvement in Vietnam
   b. Anzus
   c. SEATO
   d. United Nations
   e. NATO

3.033 The Kennedy administration was involved in: _____ .
   a. the Cuban missile crisis
   b. Pearl Harbor
   c. Vietnamization
   d. anti-Vietnam protests

3.034 The act leading the United States into military involvement in Vietnam was: _____ .
   a. the Gulf of Tonkin Resolution
   b. the sending of military advisors
   c. the commitment to Ho Chi Minh
   d. Vietnamization

Put in chronological order: Allied Strategy in World War II (each answer, 1 point).

3.035 _____ drive across France

3.036 _____ Battle of Normandy

3.037 _____ driving of Italians and Germans from North Africa

3.038 _____ closing in on Germany from the east and west

3.039 _____ invasion of Italy

Put in chronological order: American involvement after World War II (each answer, 1 point).

3.040 _____ NATO

3.041 _____ Gulf of Tonkin resolution

3.042 _____ Korean conflict

3.043 _____ United Nations

3.044 _____ Bay of Pigs

3.045 _____ Vietnamization

Answer the following question (each answer, 4 points).

3.046 What steps were taken by the Kennedy administration to resist Communist world infiltration?

_____

_____

_____

_____

_____

$\frac{60}{75}$

**Score
Adult Check**

_____

Initial   Date

Before you take the LIFEPAC Test, you may want to do one or more of these self checks.

1. _____ Read the objectives. Determine if you can do them.
2. _____ Restudy the material related to any objectives that you cannot do.
3. _____ Use the SQ3R study procedure to review the material.
4. _____ Review all activities and Self Tests and LIFEPAC Glossary.
5. _____ Restudy areas of weakness indicated by the last Self Test.